UNITED NATIONS CONFERENCE ON TRADE AND DEVELOPMENT
Geneva

INTERNATIONAL MONETARY AND FINANCIAL ISSUES FOR THE 1990s

Research papers for the Group of Twenty-Four

VOLUME VII

UNITED NATIONS
New York and Geneva, 1996

Note

Symbols of United Nations documents are composed of capital letters combined with figures. Mention of such a symbol indicates a reference to a United Nations document.

*

* *

The views expressed in this compendium are those of the authors and do not necessarily reflect the views of the UNCTAD secretariat. The designations employed and the presentation of the material do not imply the expression of any opinion whatsoever on the part of the Secretariat of the United Nations concerning the legal status of any country, territory, city or area, or of its authorities, or concerning the delimitation of its frontiers or boundaries.

*

* *

UNCTAD/GID/G.24/7

UNITED NATIONS PUBLICATION
Sales No. E.96.II.D.2
ISBN 92-1-112394-1 ISSN 1020-329X

Contents

A NEW FACILITY FOR THE IMF?

John Williamson 1

ALLOCATION OF SPECIAL DRAWING RIGHTS: THE CURRENT DEBATE

Ariel Buira and Roberto Marino 11

Abbreviations

ACP	African, Caribbean and Pacific States signatories of the Lomé Convention
ASEAN	Association of South-East Asian Nations
BIS	Bank for International Settlements
BWIs	Bretton Woods institutions
CDB	Caribbean Development Bank
CTD	Committee on Trade and Development (WTO)
DAC	Development Assistance Committee
ECU	European Currency Unit
EFTA	European Free Trade Association
ERM	Exchange Rate Mechanism
ESAF	Enhanced Structural Adjustment Facility
FAO	Food and Agriculture Organization of the United Nations
GAB	General Agreements to Borrow
GATT	General Agreement on Tariffs and Trade
GDP	gross domestic product
GNP	gross national product
GSP	Generalized System of Preferences
H-O	Heckscher-Ohlin
IBRD	International Bank for Reconstruction and Development
IDA	International Development Association
IFIs	international financial institutions
ILO	International Labour Organization
IMF	International Monetary Fund
IPRs	intellectual property rights
ITC	International Trade Centre (UNCTAD/GATT)
LIFD	low-income food deficit countries
MFA	Multi-Fibre Arrangement
MFN	most favoured nation
NAFTA	North-American Free Trade Area
NGOs	non-governmental organizations
NTBs	non-tariff barriers
OECD	Organization for Economic Co-operation and Development
RAP	Rights Accumulation Programme
SAF	Structural Adjustment Facility
SASDA	Secretariat for Analysis of Swedish Development Assistance
SDR	Special Drawing Right
SILICs	severely indebted low-income countries
SIMICs	severely indebted middle-income countries
SSA	sub-Saharan Africa
STF	Systemic Transformation Facility
TPRM	Trade Policy Review Mechanism
TRIPs	Trade-Related Intellectual Property Rights

UNCTAD	United Nations Conference on Trade and Development
UNDP	United Nations Development Programme
UNIDO	United Nations Industrial Development Organization
USAID	United States Agency for International Development
WDR	World Development Report
WFP	World Food Programme
WHO	World Health Organization
WIPO	World Intellectual Property Organization
WTO	World Trade Organization

The authors

- **Raisuddin Ahmed,** Division Director, Markets and Structural Studies Division, International Food Policy Research Institute, Washington, D.C.

- **Chandra Hardy**, Consultant Economist and Associate, International Development Training Institute, Washington, D.C.

- **Ariel Buira,** Deputy Governor, Banco de México

- **Roberto Marino,** Manager of International Economic Affairs, Banco de México

- **Dipak Mazumdar,** Adjunct Professor, Centre for International Studies, University of Toronto

- **Azizali Mohammed,** Special Adviser to the Governor, State Bank of Pakistan

- **Ann Weston,** Programme Director for Trade and Adjustment, North-South Institute, Ottawa

- **John Williamson,** Senior Fellow, Institute for International Economics, Washington, D.C.

Introduction

The Intergovernmental Group of Twenty-Four on International Monetary Affairs (G-24) was established in November 1971 to increase the negotiating strength of the developing countries in discussions that were going on at that time in the International Monetary Fund on reform of the international monetary system. Developing countries felt that they should play a meaningful role in decisions about the system, and that the effectiveness of that role would be enhanced if they were to meet regularly as a group, as the developed countries had been doing for some time in the Group of Ten (G-10).

It soon became apparent that the G-24 was in need of technical support and analysis relating to the issues arising for discussion in the Fund and Bank, including the Interim and Development Committees. In response to representations by the Chairman of the G-24 to the Secretary-General of the United Nations Conference on Trade and Development (UNCTAD), and following discussions between UNCTAD and the United Nations Development Programme (UNDP), the latter agreed in 1975 to establish a project to provide the technical support that the G-24 had requested. This was to take the form, principally, of analytical papers prepared by competent experts on issues currently under consideration in the fields of international money and finance.

Mr. Sidney Dell, a former Director in UNCTAD's Money, Finance and Development Division and subsequently Assistant Administrator of UNDP headed the project from its establishment until 1990. During this period, some 60 research papers were prepared by the Group of Twenty-Four. The high quality of this work was recognized by the Deputies and Ministers of the Group and the reports were given wide currency, some being published in five volumes by North-Holland Press and others by the United Nations.

The project work was resumed in 1990 under the direction of Professor G.K. Helleiner, Professor of Economics, University of Toronto, Toronto, Canada. The UNCTAD secretariat continues to provide both substantive and administrative backstopping to the project. Funding is currently being provided by the G-24 countries themselves, the International Development Research Centre of Canada and the Governments of Denmark and the Netherlands. As a result, it has been possible to continue to provide the Group of Twenty-Four timely and challenging analyses. These studies are being reissued periodically in compendia. This is the seventh volume to be published.

A NEW FACILITY FOR THE IMF?

John Williamson*

Abstract

This paper offers an assessment of the interests of developing countries in the proposal to create what is being referred to as a short-term financing facility within the IMF. It is argued that the more distinctive feature of such a facility is that it should be fast-disbursing. While such a facility might be helpful to industrial countries seeking to defend pegged exchange rates, the main focus of the paper is on its role in helping emergent borrowers defend themselves in the event of a liquidity crisis. The paper argues that the main interest of those G-24 member countries that might have access to such a facility is in ensuring that it would work. This would require (a) that countries have the possibility of negotiating a line of credit on which they could draw immediately in case of need - which would be conceivable only if the Fund improves its surveillance to avoid the error it made in the case of Mexico in 1994 where it endorsed policies that had resulted in an unsustainable current account deficit; (b) that the loans available form such a facility be large; and (c) that they be potentially available for the medium term, as in other borrowing from the Fund, rather than short-term.

The interests of those G-24 countries that would expect to draw on such a facility are different. They have a strong interest in ensuring that such a facility not preempt financial resources that would otherwise be available for the Fund's regular programmes (an interest that an addendum argues might more easily be satisfied if the new facility were financed by SDR allocations). If that condition were satisfied, they might benefit indirectly from the new facility inasmuch as this helped revive and sustain the support of major member countries for the IMF.

This paper offers an assessment of the interests of developing countries in the proposal to create what is being referred to as a short-term financing facility within the IMF. The label leaves something to be desired, inasmuch as the more distinctive feature of such a facility would probably be that it should be fast-disbursing rather than that it lend on short maturities. The paper starts by discussing the purpose of such a facility, summarizes the sort of proposals that have been advanced regarding its mode of operation, and then turns to an evaluation of the pros and cons.

I. Purpose of the proposal

Under conditions of high capital mobility, countries that receive capital inflows are vulnerable to swings of sentiment in the capital markets. If expectations were always rational, in the technical sense of being based upon the best possible forecasts of fundamentals using available information, and were independent of the opinions of other market participants, then there would be no case for having the official sector second-guess the conclusions of the market. But to the extent that markets are prone to speculative swings of mood (the phenomenon that justifies the quip that a country is creditworthy as long as others are lending to it), it may be useful to have an official presence in the market. Note that there is a convincing institutional reason that can explain why markets may behave in a herd manner

---

* The author is indebted to William Cline, Jeffrey Frankel and Morris Goldstein for helpful comments on a previous draft.

1

rather than act on longer-term, rational considerations, in that the managers of mutual funds are rewarded on a quarterly basis by comparison with their peers: a manager who missed out on the Mexican boom would have been penalized for it, while he would not necessarily have suffered from the Mexican collapse provided that his peers were caught as well.

One conception of what a new facility should attempt to do is to provide a backstop to resist speculative pressures that are not justified by the fundamentals. However, it may be argued that this would give it an unnecessarily broad brief, since the Fund's existing facilities are capable of handling many of the cases in which capital moves in what is judged to be a perverse direction. If one asks under what situations the Fund's existing arrangements are clearly inadequate, it is to deal with those cases where the need is for action so immediate that the normal operations of the IMF could not be effective. There are two, and only two, types of situation where this holds: (a) where a country is trying to defend an exchange-rate peg; and (b) where a country is so illiquid that without international help it will have no alternative but to default. In both of those situations help has to be immediate if it is to be of any use at all.

Enthusiasts for floating exchange rates naturally oppose the idea of giving countries extra help in defending pegged exchange rates. It follows that they would seek to restrict the scope of any new facility to helping indebted "emergent borrowers". Others seek to limit the scope of a new facility to countries which pose a systemic threat, on the grounds that a case for international action can be justified only if there is some type of international spillover. In practice this would tend to restrict the availability of the facility to large countries.

Hence there are a variety of purposes that might be served by a new facility. At the broadest level, it might be charged with helping countries to finance, and therefore ride out, capital flows that were judged to be unjustified by the fundamentals and therefore destabilizing. A more restricted mandate would limit it to occasions when immediate access was vital, either to defend a pegged exchange rate or to avoid a default. A still more restricted mandate would preclude use of the facility to defend an exchange rate peg. A further limit to the mandate would involve restricting access to countries whose default was judged to pose a systemic threat. Most of the discussion that follows focuses on the broad version of the proposal.

Given that the IMF was conceived with the aim of providing a lender of last resort, it is a natural candidate for the role of providing a backstop facility to deal with disequilibrating capital flows. Of course, the original purpose of the IMF was to lend to cover deficits in the current account, and Article VI specifically precluded lending to finance a capital outflow. But this Article has for long been something of a dead letter: at the very least, many of the current account deficits for which the IMF has lent have been amplified by capital outflows ("capital flight"). It is many years, if indeed it ever occurred, since the Fund exercised the right given to it by Article VI, Section 1(a), to "request a member to exercise controls to prevent...use of the general resources of the Fund" to meet a large or sustained outflow of capital. For some years now the Fund's policy has rather been to encourage liberalization of the capital as well as the current account.

II. The proposal

The idea of creating a short-term facility to counter capital flows judged to be speculative and destabilizing harks back to an idea that was discussed during the Committee of Twenty. It was revived by Michel Camdessus in speeches in May and June 1994. Some tentative proposals were laid out in a paper presented to the IMF Executive Board entitled "Short-Term Financing Facility" dated 26 September 1994 (subsequently referred to as "IMF paper"). It is these proposals that are summarized here. They are presented under five headings: the countries that should have access to such a facility, the terms of access, the level of access, maturity, and the source of finance for the facility.

The IMF paper contains no explicit discussion of which countries would have access to the facility, but it is clearly addressed to those member countries that have a high level of involvement in the international capital market. It appears to be addressed to the broadest conception of the purposes of such a facility, as discussed above. One can assume that the 49 countries listed in Table 1 of the IMF paper are judged to be potential candidates for access to the facility. These 49 countries comprise 22 industrial countries; 12 Latin American countries (including the seven largest countries); the Republic of Korea and the five large ASEAN countries; Egypt, Israel, Jordan, Morocco, Tunisia, and Turkey; Hungary and Poland; and South Africa. Since the paper explicitly cites it as a country that might have used such a facility had it been available in January 1993, it is surprising that the Czech Republic is not included in the list. Another country that is not included, but whose growing involvement in the international capital market might well make it a candidate for access, is India.

Since the rationale of creating a new facility is to give the IMF the capacity to provide rapid access to funds that could be used to counter speculative disturbances, the terms of access are crucial. The IMF paper proposed that a request for the right to borrow under the facility should be made at the time of an Article IV consultation. The Board would approve the availability of a line of credit for a specified period, perhaps six months, if after a comprehensive review of the country's policies it was determined that "(i) the member had a strong record of economic policies and performance and it was suggested that policies would remain appropriate; and (ii) the member was judged not to have a fundamental balance of payments problem."

The IMF paper envisaged two possible procedures under which a drawing might be made under such a line of credit. The first would give the country an automatic right to draw (at least a first tranche), with an immediate report to the Board but no need for Board approval of the drawing. The second procedure would require approval at the time of the request for use of the facility, which "would be approved if in the Fund's assessment: (i) the member's balance of payments problem was short-term; (ii) the member's economic policies had been appropriate since the last Article IV consultation; and (iii) the member was taking appropriate measures to address its short-term balance of payments difficulties." The first approach would provide more confidence to a member that it would be able to use the facility should the need arise and would in that event permit immediate access to the facility, and would therefore have more potential to reassure the markets; but it would expose the Fund to more risk. Conversely, the second approach would better protect the Fund, but at the cost of introducing uncertainty and delay into the process of approving a drawing, especially when the IMF felt that it was necessary for the country to make a policy change before a drawing was appropriate.

The IMF paper suggested that a country for which such a line of credit had been approved might be expected to report regularly a handful of key financial variables to the IMF as long as the line of credit was available. It declared that performance criteria and phased drawings would not be

appropriate, but suggested that there might be a role for tranching (i.e. that requests for drawings beyond a certain level could trigger consultations or a review of policies). Periodic consultations would be expected as long as credit was outstanding under the facility.

The IMF paper points out that the level of access would need to be commensurate with the size of reserve losses that countries can sustain over short periods if the facility was to make a useful contribution to easing the problem of destabilizing capital flows. It explicitly argues that it would be undesirable for the facility to finance shocks fully, and it assumes that because of Article VI the facility should not be used to finance a large or sustained outflow of capital. (If it had said "large and sustained", or just "sustained", this would have been unexceptionable, but the whole purpose of the facility is to finance large outflows. Indeed, it is difficult to see how such a facility can be reconciled with the present wording of Article VI.) The paper also argues that the facility should play a signalling/catalytic role that would help to reduce the magnitude of the reserve losses that would need to be financed - although the Mexican experience suggests that one should not take it for granted that Fund programs will be successful in inducing a reflux of private capital. After listing these imponderables, the IMF paper mentions a possible access range between 100 and 300 per cent of quota.

That would have given Mexico access to an IMF loan of a maximum of $7.8 billion, the figure that the Fund initially volunteered. That figure was subsequently supplemented by a further $10 billion, in an impressive display of the Fund's ability to escape from its customary constraints when it judges the case to be compelling enough. But even that total of $17.8 billion was little over a third of the total package that Mexico was judged to need. Thus the Mexican case would suggest that any useful facility will need to allow for the possibility of access on a substantially larger scale than the Fund was anticipating last September. Similarly, 300 per cent of quota would be fairly modest in comparison to the exchange market pressures that developed in the European Monetary System during its 1992-1993 crisis: the Bundesbank has stated that DM 188 billion (some $129 billion) was spent in defending the parities of European Exchange Rate Mechanism in the second half of 1992, a period during which the parities of six countries (Denmark, Ireland, Italy, Portugal, Spain, and the United Kingdom) with total IMF quotas of some $23 billion came under attack. There were, of course, other sources of funds used in intervention besides drawings on the Bundesbank.

The IMF paper proposed that the maturity of the loans under the facility would be short. A basic maturity of three months was suggested, with the possibility of rolling over for a further three months. Of course, it was recognized that a problem might turn out to be less transitory than had originally been anticipated: the IMF paper suggested that this could be met by funding via a stand-by or extended arrangement. However, it was emphasized that the facility should not be used to provide bridging finance where the need for longer term financing was apparent from the outset.

Once again, the experience with Mexico must make one doubt whether such a short-term facility would meet the need. What Mexico needed was the ability to fund a large volume of short-term into medium-term debt, which required at least the possibility of medium-term support.

As far as the financing of the facility is concerned, the paper suggested that this might be provided from the Fund's normal resources, including the possibility of activating the General Arrangements to Borrow (GAB), provided that access under the facility were within the existing limits on annual access for stand-by and extended arrangements. Since the Mexican precedent has suggested that a useful facility would require access much above those limits, however, it seems likely that the IMF would have to develop an alternative source of financing should the proposal materialize.

III. Evaluation

Clearly, members of the G-24 will need to evaluate their interests differently depending on whether or not they could expect to be eligible to draw from such a facility in the next few years. I shall consider first the interests of those countries that could expect to be eligible (see preceding section for a list of these), and subsequently of other countries.

A. *Interests of potential participants*

The dominant consideration for potential participants would presumably be whether an IMF facility of the type proposed would work. It would clearly have a limited role: it could not be expected to save a country that has a serious balance of payments problem, and indeed its availability to a country in that situation could make things worse rather than

better. This is because aid is a two-edged sword: while it can be enormously valuable in giving adjustment measures time to take effect, thus mitigating the need that would otherwise arise to resort to unnecessarily savage deflationary actions, it can also provide an unfortunate opportunity to delay adjustment if it is provided before adequate measures have been adopted. Similarly, if a country were given access to the facility when its balance of payments position was unsustainable and before it had implemented adequate adjustment measures, the facility could simply provide it with the leeway to perpetuate the unsustainable for rather longer, intensifying the ultimate pain when adjustment could no longer be delayed. Thus a key requirement for the facility to function effectively is that the IMF be able to diagnose whether or not the balance-of-payments position is sustainable.

Unfortunately, it is clear that the Fund's recent analysis has not been up to the mark. Many economists outside the IMF were on record as being concerned about the unsustainability of Mexico's policies in 1993-1994, and the threat posed by rising United States interest rates. Yet, apparently the IMF was complacent about the size of the current-account deficit that had developed, despite an anaemic growth rate, and the absence of any reason for expecting that the deficit would decline substantially without a real devaluation. The only obvious reason for imagining Mexico's policy stance to have been sustainable was the belief that its fiscal accounts were in surplus coupled with acceptance of the "Lawson thesis" that current account deficits do not matter if they are the counterpart to a deficit by the private rather than the public sector. But both elements of that argument were wrong. The Lawson thesis is erroneous in emphasizing the public/private counterpart to a deficit rather than whether it is being used to finance investment rather than consumption. Note that the thesis has failed every time it has been advanced: in Chile in 1981, in the United Kingdom in 1988, and in Mexico in 1994. Second, it turned out that Mexico actually had a less solid fiscal position than appeared, since public sector capital spending had been moved off-budget into the Development Bank several years ago when it was so compressed that no one noticed, but it had grown again to 4.1 per cent of GDP by 1994, without the IMF objecting.

However, rumours suggest that the IMF has learned from the Mexican debacle that current-account deficits do matter. While any rule of prudence limiting the size of current-account deficits judged sustainable is bound to be somewhat arbitrary, it would be better to have an arbitrary limit of, say, 3 per cent of GDP than to have no specific limit at all. There should be some scope for making such a rule a little more sophisticated than a flat limit applicable to all countries, e.g. by allowing a larger current account deficit where it is financed by inflows of direct investment, by allowing a higher limit for a country with a rapid underlying rate of growth, and/or by allowing a larger deficit for a country with a low stock of debt or a high level of exports relative to GDP. But one should certainly demand that the IMF incorporate some reasonable limits on current account deficits into its judgments about sustainability before giving it the authority to approve automatic access to lines of credit to meet a speculative outflow. Unless and until a country had adopted adjustment measures designed to reduce the deficit to the sustainable range, a country with an excessive deficit should be ineligible. Mexico should not have been pre-approved in 1994 when its current account deficit was unsustainable and there were no policy measures in place to reduce it.

Within the limited range of cases for which such a facility might be relevant, its usefulness would depend on the answers to the following questions:

(1)　Would it be possible to provide funds fast enough to nip a crisis in the bud?

(2)　Would the facility be large enough?

(3)　Would the maturity of loans be long enough to nurture the reestablishment of confidence?

The question of the speed with which funds are provided is crucial. In order to be useful, a special facility would need to be able to provide funds considerably more rapidly than has been traditional. The suggestion in the IMF paper was that this could be accomplished by pre-establishing at the time of an Article IV consultation access, or potential access, to a line of credit, provided that the IMF were satisfied that the country's policies merited support. Subsequent access to that line of credit in the event of need might be automatic or might require Fund approval.

Automatic access would clearly be an advantage in terms of permitting timely access when market pressures develop. Indeed, in the cases that some argue provide the only rationale for creating a new facility, where speed is crucial if assistance is to be of any use at all, automatic access would seem to be essential. This is because it seems inevitable that a requirement that the Fund approve a drawing on a line of credit would involve a significant delay before a drawing were possible. Admittedly, there is no very obvious

reason why IMF procedures need be as slow as they are, and the speed with which the IMF moved in the Mexican case reinforces doubts as to whether it would not be possible to do better. Macroeconomic management is by now pretty familiar intellectual terrain. On the other hand, the Managing Director's commitment in advance of consultations with the Executive Board provoked strong protests from some of the European countries. It would seem difficult to envisage a drawing taking place in much less than a month from the time a country recognizes that it faces a need unless that right is automatic. And a delay of a month gives a lot of time for financial markets to magnify a crisis.

It will be objected that a requirement of prior authorization would impose great demands on the Fund's analytical capacity to judge whether or not a country's policies are sustainable. Had the Fund erred by giving Mexico an automatic right to draw prior to 20 December 1994, it is entirely likely that the crisis would have been postponed a few weeks and would subsequently have proved even more intractable because the inherited stock of indebtedness would have been bigger. In fact, however, the difference in analytical requirements is quite limited. If the IMF had to make a quick decision at the time that a country needed to draw, it would still need to make judgments about whether policies were adequate and the balance of payments was sustainable: it would simply avoid the potential embarrassment of seeing a country that it had declared to be sound being judged by the markets to be risky, without having the chance to think again before it provided support. But if one believes that the IMF is capable of making sound judgments, and leading rather than following the markets, then it is really not obvious that it will be in a markedly better position to make such judgments at the time the country needs to draw than a few months before. If the country is required to provide the Fund with key financial statistics which give assurance that its policy stance is indeed that which was endorsed at the time the line of credit was approved, the risks in automatic access ought not to be significantly greater than those involved in a decision at the time a drawing is made. It would be a tragedy if the Fund's blindness to the unsustainability of Mexico's policies, which easily could be and hopefully already has been remedied, were to preclude the facility being designed in such a way as to be useful.

The second question is that of the size of the facility. The Mexican experience made it transparently clear that in order to address this type of need the resources to be made available have to be much larger than those which have traditionally been provided by the Fund, or that were envisaged by the IMF paper of September 1994. The additional resources that would be needed might come from several sources: from an expansion in the size of the Fund's regular resources; from an expansion in the size of commitments to the GAB, and/or an increase in the number of countries that contribute to the GAB; from an alternative GAB-like facility that might be created for this specific purpose; or from a decision to borrow in the financial markets, as recently suggested by Lamberto Dini. It would make little difference to borrowers as to where the funds came from, except insofar as potential participants might be expected to contribute relatively more under some proposals than others, with the presumption being that they would contribute the most if the facility were financed by a tailor-made GAB-like arrangement. But even this would not be a matter of much consequence to them, since the borrowings would doubtless remain liquid and the IMF pays market interest rates on its borrowing comparable to what a country can earn by holding reserves in other forms.

The final question is that of maturity. It has already been argued that the Mexican experience shows that the initial IMF proposal of a short-term facility would not be very useful. A longer-term facility could, of course, have a requirement for early repayment keyed to the reflow of reserves, so that the average expected maturity might be quite short, but any facility that has an unconditional requirement of repayment in a very short time-frame seems unlikely to be able to help restore confidence except in the easy cases where this awaits some exogenous event (like the approval of NAFTA in November 1993).

B.   Interests of non-participants

The interests of countries that would not participate in the new facility involve largely different issues. Of course, a facility that permitted countries that borrowed from it to ride out unjustified speculative pressures would also have some spillover benefits for non-participants, inasmuch as avoidance of unnecessary deflationary adjustment in those countries would help to maintain higher demand for imports (and thus of exports from other developing countries). But there are at least two other issues that seem likely to be of greater significance to those that would not themselves expect to participate.

The first of these issues is whether the new facility would crowd out other lending activities of

the IMF. Clearly, this is much more likely if it were financed from the Fund's regular resources than if special arrangements were made to borrow from some other source, either the GAB, the potential participants in the facility in a separate GAB-like arrangement, or the market. This would be of special importance if the maturity were much longer than envisaged by the IMF paper, which was argued above to be essential if the facility is to be effective. Thus other developing countries would seem to have a very clear interest in ensuring that, if such a facility comes into being, it be provided with its own distinctive source of finance rather than draw on the Fund's regular resources, and that it be financed in a way that does not require non-participating developing countries to contribute.

The other issue that surely impinges on non-participants is whether the creation of such a facility might provide a mechanism for reinvigorating the IMF. It is a weakness of the IMF that since the mid-1970s it has provided rather little in the way of services that its major shareholders find of any direct value: they have not borrowed from it, nor has there been any effective IMF input into producing mutual consistency among their macroeconomic policies. The main benefits that they perceive themselves to derive from their participation in the IMF are to have an institution to deal cooperatively with systemic problems like debt and the transition and to provide a collective international response to countries that require international support in order to get back on their feet. Having the IMF meet a systemic need for a backstop facility to stabilize the process of investment in emergent markets, or even more to help fulfil agreed exchange-rate commitments on the part of industrial countries, might help maintain their support for the institution. Such support would seem to be in the interest of developing countries, inasmuch as they are now the borrowers from the Fund and the recipients of its technical assistance.

The adoption of a backstop facility might even provide an occasion for extending the scope of effective surveillance beyond the countries that borrow from the IMF. This is because it would introduce the Fund into the business of asking whether its members' policies are sustainable even when they are not seeking to borrow immediately. Essentially the same principles that are needed to evaluate whether a country can safely be given access to a line of credit could be used to evaluate the policies of the major industrial countries. It might therefore be a relatively small additional step to introduce effective surveillance over the countries of major systemic significance, with the hope that might offer of improving their macro-economic management.

If there is felt to be a need for backstop finance and the IMF is not chosen as the vehicle for providing it, one would assume that the BIS or the G-7 would be called on to fulfil that role. The BIS has in the past provided only bridging finance, so that its acceptance of this role would be a major departure. In either event, developing countries would be deprived of any input into the determination of how much help is provided and on what conditions. Individual countries that sought help would have to negotiate bilaterally with the G-7 or the BIS, neither of which have any developing-country participation, such as one hopes provides a relatively sympathetic environment within the IMF.

IV. Conclusions

The role envisaged for a backstop facility of the character discussed in this paper is necessarily limited, to cases where the balance-of-payments position is sustainable but not so solid as to preclude the emergence of speculative pressures in response to unexpected developments. This will typically mean countries with current-account deficits in the range of 1 to perhaps 4 per cent of GDP, or with larger deficits but where remedial adjustment measures have already been implemented and the Fund is satisfied that the deficit is in the course of declining to a sustainable level. If the facility were also used to provide resources to help defend pegged exchange rates, it would similarly be crucial to develop and utilize techniques for estimating equilibrium exchange rates, and avoid lending to defend disequilibrium rates. Given the uncertainty involved in such estimations, this would imply restricting support to countries operating with a wide band for their exchange rates.

Quite a large number of developing countries, including many of the larger ones, might be eligible to draw on such a facility. Their interest is primarily in judging whether such a facility could work. This depends upon the IMF learning the lesson of the Mexican crisis, that large current account deficits are presumptively dangerous, and showing greater awareness of that in the future than it has done in the immediate past. It also requires that any facility be automatically available once a line of credit has been approved, upon the finance made available being on a scale substantially greater than the IMF has been providing in recent years, and upon maturities being

decidedly longer than was envisaged in the IMF paper of September 1994.

The interests of the remaining developing countries, those that still have little access to the international capital market and that accordingly are unlikely to be candidates for drawing on any such facility for the foreseeable future, are different. They certainly have a strong interest in ensuring that, if such a facility is developed, it has its own source of financing and does not lead to a squeeze on the funds available to them under the Fund's existing facilities. Provided that condition is met, however, it might be advantageous to them to have such a facility developed within the context of the IMF, since this would help to keep the institution alive and might help to increase its role in areas such as surveillance of the larger countries. The larger scale on which such a facility would have to operate in order to be effective might even create precedents to which non-participants could subsequently appeal in arguing for larger access limits under the Fund's existing facilities.

However, even if one does not take the traditional concerns about moral hazard very seriously[1], it may seem unlikely that the industrial countries will be willing to endorse the conditions that have been suggested above as being essential in order to allow such a facility to operate effectively. Most problems of capital flows can probably be addressed through the Fund's existing facilities, and it may be judged an over-reaction to create a new facility to deal with the occasional case where a threat of default could arise in the absence of immediate disbursement. Perhaps it would be better to think of some other way of containing that particular threat.

The most promising alternative approach would seem to be that being urged by Jeffrey Sachs, who has recently been developing proposals for giving the IMF a duty and a capacity to respond to debt difficulties by operating an international analogue to the Chapter 11 proceedings in the United States bankruptcy code ("The IMF and Economies in Crisis", mimeo). To prevent a Government that has decided to undertake reforms from being pushed into a vicious circle, in which the erosion of the State's fiscal capacity emasculates its ability to supply basic services which in turn undermines the willingness of the populace to respect the authority of the State and pay their taxes, Sachs argues that it needs the same elements as in a financial restructuring under Chapter 11 of the United States bankruptcy code. These involve "a debt service standstill at the outset of reforms; fresh working capital during restructuring, so that critical governmental functions don't collapse; and (usually) some debt reduction at the culmination of reforms, to help reestablish the Government's solvency".

It can be argued that the IMF already has the legal authority to impose a debt-service standstill, by invoking the provisions of Article VI of the IMF. The fresh working capital during restructuring is already in principle provided by the Fund's lending programs (although, Sachs argues, typically on too modest a scale). Extensive debt reconstruction, involving both debt reduction and a stretching of maturities, was negotiated for a number of countries under the Brady Plan, albeit without the assurance that a legal basis would have provided for enforcing acceptance by recalcitrant creditors. Thus the idea of turning the

IMF into an agency responsible for administering bankruptcy-style proceedings where countries find themselves impossibly illiquid does not appear entirely fanciful. Moreover, market knowledge that this was likely to happen if a country overborrowed might provide a useful discipline discouraging the markets from pouring excessive funds into emergent markets as has tended to happen in recent years.

Notes

1   What country would deliberately risk getting itself into a situation like that in which Mexico now finds itself because of a belief that this would entitle it to some bail-out finance?

Addendum

In his speech to the Social Summit in Copenhagen on 7 March 1995, the Managing Director of the IMF mentioned study of "the role the SDR could play in putting in place a last-resort financial safety net for the world". A Reuters report of 21 March 1995 on forthcoming Executive Board discussions on increases of IMF resources stated that "Camdessus has suggested resurrecting a Japanese proposal made a few years ago to set up a new IMF loan facility of up to $30 billion to help countries facing liquidity crises", which suggests that this proposal is being pursued within the IMF.

The intellectual antecedents of the idea go much further back than a Japanese proposal of few years ago. In the 1970s the then Research Director of the Fund, Jacques Polak, pointed out the simplification in the Fund's operations that could be effectuated if the General Account were to operate exclusively in SDRs. Before that, the proposals of Robert Triffin to reform the IMF so as to allow it to increase liquidity (*Gold and the Dollar Crisis*, 1959) had envisaged this being done partly by open-market operations in which the IMF would buy securities in the money markets of major members and partly by allowing the Fund to extend loans to countries that needed to borrow from it. Earlier still, the Keynes Plan for an International Clearing Union had envisaged that bancor would be created automatically as credits on the books of surplus countries as deficit countries drew on their credit lines. So the basic idea goes back a long way.

Given that the world has a fiduciary reserve asset created by the IMF, nothing could be more natural, or technically more simple, than to use it to finance lender-of-last-resort activities by a backstop facility of the character discussed in the main paper. This way of financing the facility might also overcome the main objection that was identified to such a facility from the standpoint of G-24 members, namely the danger that it would crowd out the normal lending activities of the IMF by competing for the limited pool of the Fund's financial resources. On the contrary, a decision to finance a new facility by the creation of additional SDRs might lead on in due course to a funding of all the Fund's lending by SDR creation, with the possibility this would offer of expansion in the resources available for other activities. (Of course, the fear of this effect may induce the financially conservative members of the Fund to oppose the proposal.)

The question arises as to whether the proposal is consistent with the IMF Articles of Agreement. The principle for allocating SDRs that is enshrined in Article XVIII, Section 2(b), reads:

> The rates at which allocations are to be made shall be expressed as percentages of quotas on the date of each decision to allocate ... The percentage shall be the same for all participants.

No alternative basis for allocation is provided for in the Articles. It is therefore clear that a facility of indeterminate size would not be compatible with Article XVIII. What might be legal would be to create, once-for-all, a $30 billion facility by having every member, or all the members that would be eligible to draw, assign their share of an allocation to the facility. Obviously those G-24 members that do not expect to draw would have an interest in ensuring that only countries that did expect to draw would be required to assign their share of the allocation: under such a formula they might even receive an allocation that otherwise would not happen.

This formulation recalls the many ingenious proposals that have been advanced over the years for enabling deserving groups of countries to receive new SDR allocations in the absence of a general allocation. The basic idea has always been that some countries should pass on their new allocations to the group that it was desired to favour. None of these proposals has ever won approval: they require not only the willingness of 85 per cent of the IMF voting power to approve an allocation, but unanimous consent on the part of the members expected to assign their allocations.

The alternative to achieving such unanimity would be to amend the Articles of Agreement, which is an equally daunting task.

ALLOCATION OF SPECIAL DRAWING RIGHTS: THE CURRENT DEBATE

Ariel Buira and
Roberto Marino*

Abstract

The discussion centres on the method and size of a new SDR allocation. The G-7 countries propose a selective allocation of around SDR 12-16 billion that would benefit mainly the new member countries of the Fund. The developing countries and the Managing Director of the IMF propose a general allocation of SDR 30-36 billion following the traditional method of allocating SDRs. Neither proposal can be approved without the support of the other group.

In recent years the case in favour of an SDR allocation has been based on the following considerations: (1) the econometric and empirical evidence that the demand for reserves will grow substantially during the coming years; (2) the reserve stringency faced by a large part of the Fund membership that are undertaking stabilization and transformation efforts; (3) it poses virtually no risk of affecting the global rate of inflation; (4) an SDR allocation would help advance the objective of making the SDR the principal reserve asset of the international monetary system.

In spite of these arguments and the fact that the creation of SDRs has no cost for the world economy an important group of industrial countries have opposed an SDR allocation on the grounds that it would be inflationary and that there is no long-term global liquidity need to supplement international reserves. Nevertheless, this group of countries has recently supported a special or selective SDR allocation to include the new member countries that have never participated in the SDR account.

The two proposals contain an across the board allocation and a selective allocation element. The main differences lie in the method used to effect the allocations and in the amounts involved. For the developing countries a recognition of global need and, therefore, a general allocation element is indispensable. For the G-7, accepting a general allocation without the existence of global need as perceived by them, would mean opening the door to many future allocations.

I. Introduction

During the Interim Committee meeting in October 1994 in Madrid, the issue of SDR allocations was intensely debated but no agreement was reached. The discussion centred on the method and size of the allocation. The G-7 countries proposed a selective SDR allocation of around SDR 12-16 billion that would benefit mainly the new member countries of

* The views expressed are those of the authors, they do not necessarily represent the views of the institution the authors are affiliated with.

the Fund. On their part, the developing countries and the Managing Director of the IMF proposed a general allocation of SDR 30-36 billion which constitutes the traditional method of allocating SDRs, i.e. across the board and in proportion to quotas. The G-7 proposal needed the support of developing countries since it required an amendment to the Articles of Agreement which in turn requires an 85 per cent majority of the voting power. Similarly, the developing countries' proposal needed the support of the G-7 countries since, again, an SDR allocation requires an 85 per cent majority of the voting power. A compromise was not reached since both groups argued that issues of principle and precedent were at stake. Thus, under these conditions, an impasse developed and the Committee members requested the Chairman to conduct further consultations and to call a meeting of the Committee when he judges that the prospects for the resolution of these issues are favourable.

The aim of this paper is, first, to provide a brief background on the issue of SDR allocations; second, to present and analyze the alternative proposals put forward by the G-7 countries and the developing countries, identifying the common ground and the main differences; third, to evaluate in this context some of the outstanding issues such as the merits of a general allocation versus a selective allocation, and the appropriate size of the allocation; and finally, to explore possible options around which a compromise solution might be built during the next Interim Committee meeting in Washington in April 1995.

II. Background

Agreement to allocate SDRs has been reached on only two occasions. The first one was just after the SDRs were created at the end of the sixties when it was decided to allocate SDR 9.5 billion during 1970-1972 in three instalments. The second occasion was in the late seventies when SDR 12 billion were allocated again in three instalments over 1979-1981. Currently, the total allocation of SDRs amounts to 21.4 billion or 14.8 per cent of quotas. Since no allocations have made since 1981, the SDR/ reserve ratio has fallen from a peak of 8.4 per cent in 1972 to 2.6 per cent in December 1994 (see charts 1 and 2 and annex table 1).

SDR allocations are based on the criteria set forth in Article XVIII section 1 (A) of the IMF Articles of Agreement which states:

> In all its decisions with respect to the allocation and cancellation of special drawing rights the Fund shall seek to meet the long-term global need, as and when it arises, to supplement existing reserve assets in such a manner as will promote the attainment of its purposes and will avoid economic stagnation and deflation as well as excess demand and inflation in the world.

Additionally, under Article VIII section 7 and Article XXII members are required to collaborate with the Fund toward the objective of "making the special drawing right the principal reserve asset in the international monetary system".

Since the collapse of the Bretton Woods System, there has been substantial opposition to SDR allocations by the major IMF shareholders. They argue that the expansion of international credit markets have made questionable the assumptions on which the SDR mechanism was created. A particularly contentious issue has been the criterion of long-term global need stated in Article XVIII. Developing countries argue that the criteria of long-term global need does not imply that all countries have to face reserve inadequacies - a virtually impossible condition to meet. A correct interpretation of the criterion of long-term global need requires member countries to make a judgment on whether failure to supplement reserves would have an adverse impact on the world economy and the functioning of the international monetary system. This criterion would be met when a sufficiently important group of countries are facing reserve stringencies. During the negotiations that led to the 1979-1981 SDR allocation, the Managing Director of the IMF argued in support of this view: "While it is true that most countries have a means for satisfying their need for reserves when international capital markets are free as they are today, the decision to allocate special drawing rights does not depend on a finding that the long-term global need cannot be met except by allocation" (de Vries, 1985, Vol. III, pp. 275-276).

Nevertheless, since the last allocation, the Managing Director and the staff of the IMF, as well as the majority of the Executive Directors which represent a large number of member countries, have been unable to convince the major shareholders that a new allocation of SDRs is fully justified. This small group of countries with a large voting power argue that they have not been convinced that there exists a "long-term global need" to supplement reserve assets.

III. The case for an SDR allocation

In recent years the case in favour of an SDR allocation has been based on the following considerations:

(1) There is ample econometric and empirical evidence that the demand for reserves will grow by several hundred billion dollars during the coming years in line with the growth of world trade and international capital transactions. On the basis of the projected increase in the value of world trade alone, the demand for non-gold

Chart 1

TOTAL SDR NET CUMULATIVE ALLOCATION
AS A PERCENTAGE OF QUOTA

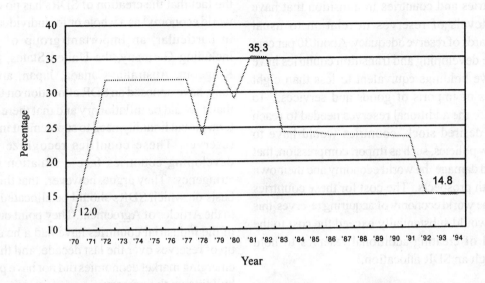

Source: IMF, *International Financial Statistics* (CD-Rom), March 1995.

Chart 2

TOTAL SDR NET CUMULATIVE ALLOCATION AS A PERCENTAGE
OF TOTAL RESERVES MINUS GOLD

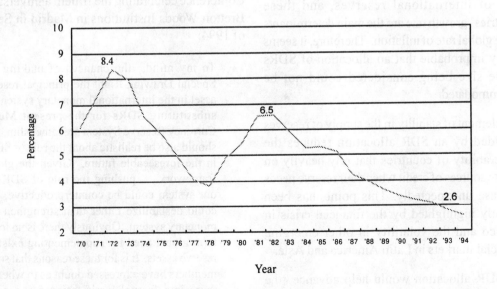

Source: IMF, *International Financial Statistics* (CD-Rom), March 1995.

reserves would increase by about SDR 400 billion over the next five years.[1]

(2) Of the total increase in the demand for reserves, an important part will correspond to developing countries and countries in transition that have low levels of reserves in relation to usual standards of reserve adequacy. About 30 per cent of the developing and transition countries have reserve holdings equivalent to less than eight weeks of imports of goods and services. To acquire the additional reserves needed to reach their desired stock, countries would have to follow policies, such as import compression, that would damage the world economy and their own growth prospects. The cost for these countries and the world economy of acquiring reserves this way would substantially exceed the cost to the world of creating additional reserves to hold through an SDR allocation.[2]

(3) The reserve stringency faced by a large part of the IMF members that are undertaking substantial stabilization and transformation efforts increases the risk of widespread programme setbacks or failures. An SDR allocation would help alleviate this reserve stringency and therefore facilitate the adjustment process.

(4) An SDR allocation of the size being contemplated poses virtually no risk of affecting the global rate of inflation. The liabilities of the main industrial countries, which constitute the bulk of international reserves, and these countries' growth rate are the main determinants of the global rate of inflation. Therefore, it seems highly improbable that an allocation of SDRs of the size being considered could not be accommodated.

(5) The element of stability in the supply of reserves provided by an SDR allocation reduces the vulnerability of countries that rely heavily on private sources of credit when their reserve needs increase unexpectedly. This point has been recently highlighted by the financial crisis in Mexico and the volatility in other emerging financial markets in Latin America and Asia.

(6) An SDR allocation would help advance the objective of making the SDR the principal reserve asset of the international monetary system as mandated in the Articles of Agreement of the IMF.

IV. The arguments against an SDR allocation

In spite of the above mentioned arguments and the fact that the creation of SDRs has no cost for the world economy[3] as a whole or for individual countries in particular, an important group of countries, including Germany, the United States, the United Kingdom, Australia, Canada, Japan, and recently Italy, have opposed an SDR allocation on the grounds that it would be inflationary and that there is no long-term global liquidity need to supplement international reserves. These countries recognize that most developing countries face a situation of reserve stringency. They argue, however, that this is not the basis on which SDRs should be allocated according to the Articles of Agreement. They point out that most of the industrial countries have had a healthy build-up of reserves over the last decade, and that recently emerging market economies did not have problems in building up their reserves.

Germany is particularly worried that an SDR allocation at this juncture could create a precedent. It is feared that regular SDR allocations would revitalize an international monetary asset whose creation does not depend on the policies of a central bank of an industrialized country; this would pose an inflationary danger to the world economy.

A clear example of the German point of view regarding the role of the SDR are the remarks by Hans Tietmeyer, President of the Bundesbank, at the Conference celebrating the fiftieth anniversary of the Bretton Woods Institutions in Madrid in September of 1994:

> To my mind, the chances of making the Special Drawing Right the principal reserve asset in the international monetary system by substituting SDRs for the present Multi-Currency Reserve System are rather slim. We should also be realistic about the role of SDRs in the foreseeable future. Given the global framework ..., pushing the role of SDRs in our system could be counterproductive, and could destabilize rather than strengthen our monetary system. Obviously there is no long-term global need for supplementing existing reserve assets. It is for these reasons that some members have expressed doubt as to whether there is a factual justification for general allocations of SDRs in present circumstances. On the other hand, there are good reasons for being in favour of enabling the Fund's new members to participate fully in the SDR

system through a special allocation of SDRs ensuring the equitable participation of all members in the SDR mechanism (Tietmeyer, 1994).

Since an SDR allocation requires an 85 per cent majority, the above mentioned countries have succeeded in blocking a new allocation over the last decade. However, as the former Soviet Republics joined the Fund, and as is evident from the above quotations, the position of the industrial countries opposing an SDR allocation changed somewhat.

V. The current debate

Recently industrial countries have come to the view that a special or selective SDR allocation to benefit the new member countries that have never participated in the SDR account could be envisaged. Since this is not possible under the terms of the Articles of Agreement, which requires allocations to be general, an amendment of the Articles would be necessary. This, in turn, necessitates a 85 per cent majority as well as ratification by the member countries.

On their part, the developing countries opposed an amendment whose purpose was to permit a selective SDR allocation that would not benefit them and make future general allocations even more difficult. Moreover, this seemed to introduce an "ad-hoc" change in the basic law of the institution by a group of countries that wished to provide financial assistance to the former Soviet Republics without making the necessary budgetary contribution. While the developing countries favour the participation of the former Soviet Republics in the SDR system, they believe that this should be done through a general SDR allocation.

VI. Alternative proposals

A. The proposal by the United States and the United Kingdom

In view of the above, the United States and United Kingdom, subsequently supported by the G-7, proposed a compromise with the following objectives:

(1) ensure an equitable participation of all members in the SDR mechanism;

(2) provide a means of distribution which would command wider support than either a selective or a general allocation alone;

(3) limit the total new issue of SDRs to a moderate amount; and

(4) remove the requirement for a full consensus on the determination of a global need.

Following these objectives, the proposal by the United States and the United Kingdom put forward the following formula for a selective SDR allocation: each member country could choose between an allocation that raised their SDR/quota ratio to between 20 and 24 per cent, or it could receive a minimum allocation of between 6 and 8 per cent of its quota. With the 20/6 per cent combination SDR 12 billion would be allocated, and with the 24/8 per cent combination SDR 16 billion.

Following this proposal a number of conclusions emerged:

(1) As no general allocation of SDRs was warranted at present, the traditional mechanism for SDR allocation could not be used, and there would be no recognition of a global need for reserve supplementation.

(2) The so-called "issue of equity"[4] would be solved through a specific allocation by allowing those member countries that never received an allocation of SDRs to receive an allocation up to an agreed threshold (20 to 24 per cent of quota).

(3) Only a modest amount of SDRs would be allocated (12-16 billion SDRs).

(4) The minimum allocation of 6 to 8 per cent of quota to all members countries would smooth out possible reverse inequities.

Point 4, the minimum allocation element, was introduced with the clear intention of making the proposal palatable to the group of countries that already had an SDR/quota ratio near or above the threshold. This group includes many low-income countries, some large middle-income countries like India and Argentina, and, conspicuously, the United Kingdom. They believed that a minimum SDR allocation equivalent to 6 to 8 per cent of their quota for all member countries would contribute to reach a consensus, since member countries would be able to choose between the target threshold level or the minimum allocation. The allocation under the proposal would be around one-third of what had been proposed by the Managing Director, increasing the total stock of SDRs to close to SDR 34-38 billion. This proposal would, of course, require an amendment to the Articles of Agreement.

In table 2, IMF member countries are ranked according to their current SDR/quota ratio. The highest ratio is that of the United Kingdom (25.8 per cent). The United States and Canada have ratios of 18.5 per cent and 18 per cent, respectively. The IMF average (excluding those with zero allocations) is 16.1 per cent. Among the other G-7 countries the ratio ranges from 10.8 per cent for Japan to 15.8 per cent for Italy.

If the higher range of the proposal by the United States and the United Kingdom is taken as a basis, 81 countries would opt for the 8 per cent minimum, while the remaining 91 countries would receive a greater allocation by choosing the 24 per cent ratio. The average ratio for the whole IMF membership would rise to 25.8 per cent (see chart 3).

Of the total SDR 16 billion allocated under this proposal, industrial countries would be allocated around SDR 8.3 billion, and developing countries (including the former Soviet Republics accounting for SDR 1.6 billion) SDR 7.7 billion. ESAF-eligible countries would be allocated around SDR 1.8 billion. As a result, industrial countries would command 61.2 per cent of total allocations and developing countries around 38.8 per cent.[5] Thus, under the proposed distribution scheme, the countries that benefit most at the margin are the ones that have never received SDR allocations.

The developing country members of the IMF criticized the above proposal on the following grounds:

(1) The selective approach of the proposal would weaken the traditional mechanism for SDR allocation. Moreover, it avoided the term "General Allocation" for the minimum allocation element to which every country would be entitled.

(2) Since an amendment to the Articles of Agreement requires a lengthy process of ratification by member countries, this proposal would involve a delay of up to two years. The representatives of the developing countries also argued that it would be difficult for their parliaments to approve a proposal that flew in the face of the Articles of Agreement and represented little benefit to them. Indeed, the allocation of SDRs to developing countries, excluding the former Soviet Republics, would be very small, of the order of SDR 3.9 - 5.2 billion.

(3) The proposal would not lead to an "equitable" solution defined as the attainment of an equal ratio of SDR allocation to quotas for all countries.

B. *The proposal by the developing countries*

As a counter-proposal, the developing countries suggested a two-step scheme which tried to mimic the features of the proposal by the United States and the United Kingdom but incorporated elements that would make it more acceptable to the developing countries.

The main features of the developing countries' proposal are the following:

(1) An immediate general SDR allocation equivalent to 10 per cent of quotas or some 14.5 billion SDRs, similar to the 6 - 8 per cent minimum overall allocation in the proposal by the United States and the United Kingdom. This would require the recognition of a global need and would keep the traditional mechanism for SDR allocations alive.

(2) An amendment to the Articles of Agreement to allow a further selective allocation of around 16 billion SDRs that would allow all countries to reach an equal SDR/quota ratio of 35.8 per cent.[6] This would level the playing field for the countries that joined the IMF after 1981, when the last SDR allocation took place (see chart 4).

The developing countries argued that the proposal had two advantages: First, the 10 per cent general allocation would come into effect immediately since it did not require parliamentary approval. This would provide a timely relief to the reserve stringency faced by many transition economies and developing countries. Secondly, equity, which was the declared motive of the exercise, would be better served, since at the time the amendment was ratified by 85 per cent of the voting power all members could reach the same SDR/quota ratio.

As shown in chart 4 and table A2, under the developing countries' proposal (G-11 proposal), the first step is to maintain the current structure of SDR allocations. This would imply SDR allocation of SDR 5.7 billion for developing countries and SDR 8.8 billion for industrial countries. The second step would equate all countries SDR/quota ratio at 35.8 per cent implying an allocation of SDR 16 billion. Thus total SDRs allocated under this method would amount to

Chart 3

NET CUMULATIVE ALLOCATION AS A PERCENTAGE OF QUOTA ACCORDING TO THE PROPOSAL BY THE UNITED STATES AND THE UNITED KINGDOM

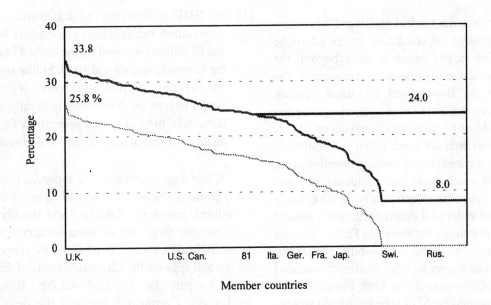

Source: IMF, *International Financial Statistics* (CD-Rom), March 1995.

Chart 4

NET CUMULATIVE ALLOCATION AS A PERCENTAGE OF QUOTA ACCORDING TO THE PROPOSAL BY THE DEVELOPING COUNTRIES

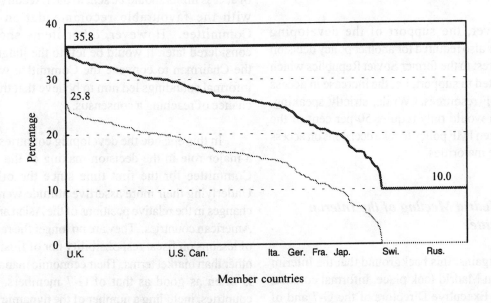

Source: IMF, *International Financial Statistics* (CD-Rom), March 1995.

around SDR 30.5 billion. This procedure would also greatly benefit the former Soviet Republics. As can be seen in table 2, the selective allocation would range from zero for the United Kingdom to 25.8 per cent for those countries that are new IMF members and those that have not participated in previous allocations.

Thus, prior to the Madrid meetings the position of the two groups of countries appeared to be polarized. The larger issues at stake beyond the numbers were related to principle and precedent. On the one hand, the Bundesbank sustained a strong opposition to any general SDR allocation arguing that the IMF should not recognize the existence of any long-term global liquidity need. Other G-7 countries, most of which have been traditionally unenthusiastic about the SDR mechanism, were reluctant to leave Germany to stand alone, particularly as the country had already shouldered a disproportionate share of the burden of providing assistance to Eastern Europe and the former Soviet Republics. Notably, the United States, which had shown signs of flexibility[7] decided to support the German position. Only France[8] which had always favoured the SDR scheme, fought against the German position but in the end seemed to cave in as well.

On the other hand, the developing countries, as well as the Managing Director, felt that perhaps for the first time in years they had a stronger negotiating position, since the G-7 required the developing-country vote not only to provide the former Soviet Republics with SDRs but also to renew the Systemic Transformation Facility, of which Russia and other economies in transition are the only direct beneficiaries.

Moreover, the support of the developing countries was also required for another policy decision of direct interest to the former Soviet Republics which the G-7 wanted to support, i.e. the increase in access limits to IMF resources. While, strictly speaking, this decision would only require 50 per cent of the vote, it has been IMF policy to take decisions on access by very large majorities.

C. *The Madrid Meeting of the Interim Committee*

It was against this background that the Interim Committee in Madrid took place. Informal contacts between the Executive Directors of the G-7 and of the developing countries indicated a possible compromise package including the following elements:

(1) a renewal of the Systemic Transformation Facility (STF);

(2) an enlargement of access limits of direct benefit to Russia and other economies in transition as well as to certain developing countries;

(3) an SDR allocation of an amount to be determined, but probably somewhere between the 16 billion proposed by the United States and the United Kingdom and the 30 billion suggested by the developing countries, with some proportion to be distributed generally and the remainder to be allocated selectively following an amendment of the Articles of Agreement.

While discussions initially appeared to confirm that a compromise solution would be reached along these lines, members of the G-7 and Russia finally indicated that there was no basis for a compromise on an SDR allocation. Therefore, they proposed to discuss and approve the various elements of the above package separately. The G-7 and the Chairman of the Interim Committee pressed the developing countries hard to unbundle the package, insisting that the renewal of the STF and the increase in access limits from 68 to 85 per cent should be approved immediately since there was no opposition, and that the issue of an SDR allocation could be postponed. The representatives of developing countries all took the position that the various issues were part of a package, highlighting the links and reminding that this was the usual G-7 negotiating strategy. Developing countries were not prepared to consider the issues separately. They finally agreed that the enlargement of access limits should be sent to the Executive Board with the favourable recommendation of the Committee. However, other items should be considered later. It would be left to the judgment of the Chairman to convene the Committee when his informal soundings led him to believe that there was chance of reaching a consensus.

In this episode the developing countries played a major role in the decision making of the Interim Committee for the first time since the oil crisis. Underlying their more assertive attitude were major changes in the relative positions of the Asian and Latin American countries. They are no longer the recipients of lessons on fiscal responsibility nor of financing in other than market terms. Their economic management is often as good as that of G-7 members. These countries, including a number of the dynamic export-led economies, had regained confidence which most had not felt since the debt crisis. They felt that the decisions of the institution should be ruled by the Articles of Agreement and that its basic law should not be changed to accommodate the political objectives of a small group of industrial countries. In the internal discussions some delegations were in favour of preserving the SDR as an instrument for the future, others argued that their parliaments would not approve an amendment in the Articles of Agreement that did not benefit them unless it were part of a wider package. Some questioned the validity and sincerity of the G-7 argument on the inflationary impact of a, say, 25 billion SDR allocation, most of which would go to the industrial countries at a time when the United States alone was running a current account deficit expected to reach $140 billion.[9] Questions could also be raised as to the motivation that led reserve currency countries to oppose the role of the SDR as a reserve asset.

Be that as it may, the failure of the Madrid meeting[10] to reach a consensus on certain decisions of direct interest to the G-7 countries provoked their anger and frustration, both with a Managing Director who, in their view, took an excessively independent position and with countries which they considered ungrateful for past assistance, as one European minister put it.

It appears that the failure of the Interim Committee to reach a more satisfactory conclusion in Madrid can, to a large extent, be attributed to the change in the position of the G-7 ministers, which clashed with the renewed confidence of the developing countries and their growing role in the world economy which led them to be more assertive and less willing than in the past to have their views disregarded.

The discussion had gone beyond the realm of technical debate and got stuck on issues of pride, principle and precedent. The G-7, led by Germany and with the possible exception of France and Italy, clearly disregarded the role of the SDR in the international monetary system. Were it not for the needs of the former Soviet Republics, the G-7 countries would probably be willing to do away with the SDR once and for all. The pressure put on individual developing countries to renew the STF before dealing with the SDR has been intense. Developing countries have continued to resist, but with the deadline for the expiration of STF approaching (15 December 1994) they agreed a limited extension of the STF from 31 December 1994 to 30 April 1995. Although this action may weaken the developing countries' negotiating position somewhat, the G-7 remain under pressure to come to a compromise on

the SDR issue during the next Interim Committee Meeting.

D. *Elements for a compromise solution*

The two proposals, that of the United States and the United Kingdom, on the one hand, and that of the developing countries on the other, have many elements in common. The proposal by the developing countries was actually designed to mimic the G-7 proposal in order to move towards a consensus. Both proposals contain an across-the-board allocation and a selective allocation element. The main differences lie in the method used to effect the allocations and in the amounts involved. For the developing countries, a recognition of global need and, therefore, a general allocation element is indispensable. In their view, the denial of global need under current circumstances would be equivalent to barring any future SDR allocation under Article XVIII. For the G-7, accepting a general allocation without the existence of global need (as they perceived it), would mean opening the door to many future allocations. They consider that at any moment in time there will be a group of countries with reserve inadequacies, and therefore, a reason to allocate SDRs.

Under these circumstances, any compromise proposal would require that both groups move beyond the positions taken on the issues of principle and precedent. There are several possible combinations that would require a certain degree of flexibility. A few options are explored below.

A first option consists in the G-7 countries revising their position on global need in return for a reduction in the amounts of SDRs to be allocated. Under this option, the general allocation element could be minimized to a symbolic figure of SDR 5 billion or 3.5 per cent of quotas, for example. The selective element would be kept untouched to permit member countries to reach a 24 per cent SDR/quota ratio. G-7 countries could argue that the bulk of the allocation is done by a selective increase to solve the perceived inequities and that the general allocation element is just a symbolic gesture to break the impasse. The developing countries might accept this solution because the principle of a general allocation is kept alive, the global need being recognized. However, the total amount of SDRs allocated would be much lower than under their own proposal.

A second option is that the developing countries cede on the principle of global need but achieve an allocation of SDRs the amount contained in their initial proposal. Under this option, the entire allocation would be based on an amendment to the Articles, with the only factor to be considered being the equalization of the SDR/quota ratio for all member countries at a level of at least 35.8 per cent. In SDR terms this would correspond exactly to the amount following from the initial proposal of the developing countries. They could argue that what matters the most is the total amount of SDRs available, while the method is of secondary importance. In any case, developing countries could recognize that future SDR allocations still depend on the volition of a small group of industrial countries. The G-7 countries could, in turn, defend this solution as a measure to solve, at a historic juncture, the perceived inequities in the SDR system for new members.

E.　New elements in the SDR discussion

The crisis in Mexico and its contagion effects on other Latin American economies and some emerging-market countries in Asia and Central Europe will undoubtedly lead to a reassessment of the adequacy of Fund resources and its capacity to deal with short-term liquidity crises. This episode of financial market turbulence illustrates that even those countries that can meet their reserve needs by borrowing from private markets face significant interest rate spreads and are highly vulnerable to sudden shifts in market sentiment. The case for owned reserves versus borrowed reserves and, therefore, the case for an SDR allocation have thus been strengthened. A significant new allocation could help restore confidence of financial markets by strengthening the reserve position of IMF member countries.

An important element of the Fund's response to the Mexican crisis was the speed with which it could support the adjustment programme and the unprecedented amount of financial resources made available to stabilize financial markets. It would be a great advance in today's world of large-scale movement of funds across borders, if the IMF could have a facility to support adequately individual countries facing severe short-term external liquidity problems.

The Managing Director of the IMF has recently floated the idea of using the SDR as a "safety net" instrument. Under this scheme, the IMF could allocate SDRs on a temporary basis to individual countries facing balance-of-payments or external liquidity problems. In crisis situations the amounts involved could be substantial. This scheme would require an amendment of the Articles, since it would not be across the board and in response to a long-term global need of the world economy. Such a role for the SDR, which would strengthen the lender-of-last-resort function of the IMF, is certainly something that should be considered. The IMF, if endowed with adequate resources, could ensure that an illiquid yet solvent member country could deal with a creditor panic. IMF lending would be prudent since a precondition would be that IMF recognizes the country as solvent. The moral hazard risks would be reduced by the conditionality linked to the temporary SDR allocation that the country adopt appropriate adjustment measures, and by lending at a penalty rate. More importantly, the creation of such support or facility, with the public knowledge of its existence, could in many cases suffice to restore the confidence that would prevent or stop a run on a currency and allow a country time to make the necessary adjustments in an orderly manner.

To sum up, it is clear that an SDR allocation is warranted, perhaps in amounts even larger than those being currently considered. It is also clear that the developing countries' arguments are strong and that they should join forces with the former Soviet Republics and staff and management of the IMF to obtain an SDR allocation that would strengthen the International Monetary System. Unfortunately, the issue is stuck in a sterile debate on principles and precedents. The options we have put forward require that at least one of the groups involved take the initiative to move from their Madrid positions, but a practical and constructive solution has to emerge. Additionally, the developing countries should press for the enhancement of the role of the SDR through the use of the SDR as a safety-net instrument. The lack of a lender of last resort is a major shortcoming of the system. Like a fire department it would benefit the international community as a whole. It would strengthen the basic principle of international monetary cooperation that is the building block of the IMF.

Notes

1　See estimates of demand for international reserves by the IMF staff and by Buira (1995).

2　The issue of whether the SDR system gives rise to a resource transfer has been extensively debated. An important distinction has to be made between the allocation itself and the net use of SDRs after the allocation. SDRs are costless to create; therefore, the allocation itself does not imply any resource transfer.

Similarly, use of SDRs to acquire another reserve asset does not imply any transfer of real resources; it is simply a swap of one reserve asset for another. However, spending the SDRs on real resources does imply a current transfer of real resources, which has to be financed by interest payments and at some point principal payments. Since the interest rate on the use of SDRs is a market rate, countries that "extend credit" to the users of SDRs are receiving a market return for such credit. The experience shows that countries with excess holdings of SDRs have willingly maintained them. Thus, their behaviour as net creditors in the SDR account shows that they are satisfied with the return on their SDR holdings. See Coats et al. (1990).

3   To the extent that SDRs remedy a liquidity shortage in a number of least developed countries they actually contribute to world economic activity and international trade.

4   It is an open question whether an issue of equity arises when new shareholders of a club (or firm) should share in the profit or benefits distributed before they become members.

5   The percentage shares in quotas between industrial countries and developing countries are 61 per cent and 39 per cent respectively.

6   Curiously, the maximum ratio of 35.8 per cent is derived from the current highest ratio of 25.8 per cent corresponding to the United Kingdom plus the 10 per cent general allocation.

7   In his speech to the Interim Committee Meeting in April 1994 the Secretary of the United States Treasury said: "I am not persuaded that there is a general shortage of reserves or liquidity in the world economy. Therefore, I see no basis for a large general allocation of SDRs". This statement signalled to some greater flexibility toward a "small" SDR allocation.

8   The French Finance Minister argued during the Interim Committee Meeting: "Some countries regretted that a general allocation could not be approved. I too would have preferred this outcome. But I also prefer a compromise to a disagreement on principles. I would observe that the selective allocation proposed by the G-7 does, in fact, benefit all countries. In this sense, it is therefore a general allocation, even if it also enables a number of historical injustices to be corrected."

9   If the United States were worried about the inflationary

dangers of excess liquidity in the world, it could follow the suggestions of the former Managing Director of the IMF Witteveen and use SDRs in partial settlement of its payments imbalances.

10   In an article of 8 October 1994, entitled "The Fight for the Fund", the *Economist* commented as follows: "A furious row between industrialized and developing countries over proposals to raise world liquidity and give more financial assistance to ex-communist countries soured the 50th anniversary gathering of the World Bank and the IMF. For the first time a united block of developing countries rejected proposals put forward by the G7 group of industrialized countries (America, Britain, Canada, France, Germany, Italy and Japan). Some participants said the fight had opened a new north-south divide. Others mused whether there was any future for the IMF. Reality is more banal: the meeting was a diplomatic disaster that can probably be sorted out once tempers cool."

References

Bretton Woods Commission (1994), "Bretton Woods: Looking to the Future", Proceedings of a Conference, 20-22 July (Washington, D.C.).

BUIRA, Ariel (1995), "Reflections on the International Monetary System", *Princeton Essays in International Finance*, No. 195 (Princeton: Princeton University Press).

COATS, Warren L., Reinhard W. FURSTENBERG, and Peter ISARD (1990), "The SDR System and the Issue of Resource Transfers, *Princeton Essays in International Finance*, No. 180 (Princeton: Princeton University Press).

DE VRIES, Margaret Garritsen (1985), *The International Monetary Fund 1972-1978; Cooperation on Trial* (Washington, D.C.: IMF).

IMF (1994), "Improving the International Monetary System: Constraints and Possibilities", *Occasional Paper*, No. 116 (Washington, D.C.), December 1994.

TIETMEYER, Hans (1994), "Establishing a Vision for Stabilization and Reform", Proceedings of the Conference of Fifty Years after Bretton Woods: The Future of the IMF and the World Bank, Session No. 8, 30 September, processed.

Annex tables

Table A1

TOTAL SDR ALLOCATIONS AND IMF QUOTAS, 1970-1994

Year	Reserves Minus gold (A)	IMF quota (B)	Net cumulative SDR allocation (C)	(C/A)	(C/B)
		(SDR million)		*(Per cent)*	
1970	56154	28433	3414	6.1	12.0
1971	87056	28808	6363	7.3	22.1
1972	110904	29169	9315	8.4	31.9
1973	116836	29189	9315	8.0	31.9
1974	144001	29189	9315	6.5	31.9
1975	158697	29211	9315	5.9	31.9
1976	186628	29213	9315	5.0	31.9
1977	228473	29219	9315	4.1	31.9
1978	245487	39011	9315	3.8	23.9
1979	272872	39017	13348	4.9	34.2
1980	321284	59596	17386	5.4	29.2
1981	329676	60674	21433	6.5	35.3
1982	327916	61060	21433	6.5	35.1
1983	362314	88509	21433	5.9	24.2
1984	407050	89302	21433	5.3	24.0
1985	404830	89305	21433	5.3	24.0
1986	418622	89988	21433	5.1	23.8
1987	507516	89988	21433	4.2	23.8
1988	542657	89988	21433	3.9	23.8
1989	590920	90133	21433	3.6	23.8
1990	637593	91103	21433	3.4	23.5
1991	671644	91153	21433	3.2	23.5
1992	692908	141404	21433	3.1	15.2
1993	756796	144800	21433	2.8	14.8
1994	820841	144938	21433	2.6	14.8

Source: IMF, *International Financial Statistics* (CD-Rom), March 1995.

SDR ALLOCATIONS AND IMF QUOTAS, BY COUNTRY

	Num.	IMF quota (A)	Net cumulative SDR allocation (B)	C=(B/A)	U.S.-U.K. proposal Option I C+8	U.S.-U.K. proposal Option II	Developing country proposal C+10	Developing country proposal Extra increase	Total
		(SDR million)			*(Per cent)*				
United Kingdom	1	7414.6	1913.1	25.8	33.8	—	35.8	—	35.8
Lao P.D. Republic	2	39.1	9.4	24.0	32.0	—	34.0	1.8	35.8
Burundi	3	57.2	13.7	24.0	32.0	—	34.0	1.8	35.8
Equatorial Guinea	4	24.3	5.8	23.9	31.9	—	33.9	1.9	35.8
Cambodia	5	65.0	15.4	23.7	31.7	—	33.7	2.1	35.8
Myanmar	6	184.9	43.5	23.5	31.5	—	33.5	2.3	35.8
Sri Lanka	7	303.6	70.9	23.4	31.4	—	33.4	2.4	35.8
Mali	8	68.9	15.9	23.1	31.1	—	33.1	2.7	35.8
Rwanda	9	59.5	13.7	23.0	31.0	—	33.0	2.8	35.8
Ghana	10	274.0	63.0	23.0	31.0	—	33.0	2.8	35.8
Chad	11	41.3	9.4	22.8	30.8	—	32.8	3.0	35.8
Sierra Leone	12	77.2	17.5	22.7	30.7	—	32.7	3.1	35.8
Iran	13	1078.5	244.1	22.6	30.6	—	32.6	3.2	35.8
Central African Rep.	14	41.2	9.3	22.6	30.6	—	32.6	3.2	35.8
Pakistan	15	758.2	170.0	22.4	30.4	—	32.4	3.4	35.8
Guinea	16	78.7	17.6	22.4	30.4	—	32.4	3.4	35.8
India	17	3055.5	681.2	22.3	30.3	—	32.3	3.5	35.8
Gambia	18	22.9	5.1	22.3	30.3	—	32.3	3.5	35.8
Uruguay	19	225.3	50.0	22.2	30.2	—	32.2	3.6	35.8
Afghanistan	20	120.4	26.7	22.2	30.2	—	32.2	3.6	35.8
Uganda	21	133.9	29.4	22.0	30.0	—	32.0	3.8	35.8
New Zealand	22	650.1	141.3	21.7	29.7	—	31.7	4.1	35.8
Malawi	23	50.9	11.0	21.6	29.6	—	31.6	4.2	35.8
Guyana	24	67.2	14.5	21.6	29.6	—	31.6	4.2	35.8
Mauritius	25	73.3	15.7	21.4	29.4	—	31.4	4.4	35.8
Tanzania	26	146.9	31.4	21.4	29.4	—	31.4	4.4	35.8
Madagascar	27	90.4	19.3	21.3	29.3	—	31.3	4.5	35.8
Burkina Faso	28	44.2	9.4	21.3	29.3	—	31.3	4.5	35.8
Bolivia	29	126.2	26.7	21.2	29.2	—	31.2	4.6	35.8
Benin	30	45.3	9.4	20.8	28.8	—	30.8	5.0	35.8
Argentina	31	1537.1	318.4	20.7	28.7	—	30.7	5.1	35.8
Senegal	32	118.9	24.5	20.6	28.6	—	30.6	5.2	35.8
Mauritania	33	47.5	9.7	20.4	28.4	—	30.4	5.4	35.8
Colombia	34	561.3	114.3	20.4	28.4	—	30.4	5.4	35.8
Nicaragua	35	96.1	19.5	20.3	28.3	—	30.3	5.5	35.8
Togo	36	54.3	11.0	20.3	28.3	—	30.3	5.5	35.8
Jamaica	37	200.9	40.6	20.2	28.2	—	30.2	5.6	35.8
Australia	38	2333.2	470.6	20.2	28.2	—	30.2	5.6	35.8
Honduras	39	95.0	19.1	20.1	28.1	—	30.1	5.7	35.8
Morocco	40	427.7	85.7	20.0	28.0	—	30.0	5.8	35.8
Egypt	41	678.4	135.9	20.0	28.0	—	30.0	5.8	35.8
Costa Rica	42	119.0	23.7	19.9	27.9	—	29.9	5.9	35.8
El Salvador	43	125.6	25.0	19.9	27.9	—	29.9	5.9	35.8
Dominican Republic	44	158.8	31.6	19.9	27.9	—	29.9	5.9	35.8
Viet Nam	45	241.6	47.7	19.7	27.7	—	29.7	6.1	35.8
Chile	46	621.7	121.9	19.6	27.6	—	29.6	6.2	35.8
Peru	47	466.1	91.3	19.6	27.6	—	29.6	6.2	35.8
Niger	48	48.3	9.4	19.5	27.5	—	29.5	6.3	35.8
Cyprus	49	100.0	19.4	19.4	27.4	—	29.4	6.4	35.8
Iceland	50	85.3	16.4	19.2	27.2	—	29.2	6.6	35.8
Paraguay	51	72.1	13.7	19.0	27.0	—	29.0	6.8	35.8

Table A2 (continued)

	Num.	IMF quota (A)	Net cumulative SDR allocation (B)	C=(B/A)	U.S.-U.K. proposal Option I C+8	U.S.-U.K. proposal Option II	C+10	Developing country proposal Extra increase	Developing country proposal Total
		(SDR million)			*(Per cent)*				
Trinidad and Tobago	52	246.8	46.2	18.7	26.7	—	28.7	7.1	35.8
Kenya	53	199.4	37.0	18.6	26.6	—	28.6	7.2	35.8
United States	54	26526.8	4899.5	18.5	26.5	—	28.5	7.3	35.8
Philippines	55	633.4	116.6	18.4	26.4	—	28.4	7.4	35.8
Cameroon	56	135.1	24.5	18.1	26.1	—	28.1	7.7	35.8
Canada	57	4320.3	779.3	18.0	26.0	—	28.0	7.8	35.8
Guatemala	58	153.8	27.7	18.0	26.0	—	28.0	7.8	35.8
Greece	59	587.6	103.5	17.6	25.6	—	27.6	8.2	35.8
Panama	60	149.6	26.3	17.6	25.6	—	27.6	8.2	35.8
Swaziland	61	36.5	6.4	17.5	25.5	—	27.5	8.3	35.8
Turkey	62	642.0	112.3	17.5	25.5	—	27.5	8.3	35.8
Syrian Arab Republic	63	209.9	36.6	17.4	25.4	—	27.4	8.4	35.8
Macedonia	64	49.6	8.4	16.9	24.9	—	26.9	8.9	35.8
Croatia	65	261.6	44.2	16.9	24.9	—	26.9	8.9	35.8
Slovenia	66	150.5	25.4	16.9	24.9	—	26.9	8.9	35.8
Congo	67	57.9	9.7	16.8	24.8	—	26.8	9.0	35.8
Malta	68	67.5	11.3	16.7	24.7	—	26.7	9.1	35.8
Denmark	69	1069.9	178.9	16.7	24.7	—	26.7	9.1	35.8
Malaysia	70	832.7	139.1	16.7	24.7	—	26.7	9.1	35.8
Ireland	71	525.0	87.3	16.6	24.6	—	26.6	9.2	35.8
Tunisia	72	206.0	34.2	16.6	24.6	—	26.6	9.2	35.8
Finland	73	861.8	142.7	16.6	24.6	—	26.6	9.2	35.8
Mexico	74	1753.3	290.0	16.5	24.5	—	26.5	9.3	35.8
Brazil	75	2170.8	358.7	16.5	24.5	—	26.5	9.3	35.8
Barbados	76	48.9	8.0	16.4	24.4	—	26.4	9.4	35.8
Yemen	77	176.5	28.7	16.3	24.3	—	26.3	9.5	35.8
Venezuela	78	1951.3	316.9	16.2	24.2	—	26.2	9.6	35.8
South Africa	79	1365.4	220.4	16.1	24.1	—	26.1	9.7	35.8
Israel	80	666.2	106.4	16.0	24.0	—	26.0	9.8	35.8
Indonesia	81	1497.6	239.0	16.0	24.0	—	26.0	9.8	35.8
Côte d'Ivoire	82	238.2	37.8	15.9	—	24.0	25.9	9.9	35.8
Belgium	83	3102.3	485.3	15.6	—	24.0	25.6	10.2	35.8
Nepal	84	52.0	8.1	15.6	—	24.0	25.6	10.2	35.8
Lesotho	85	23.9	3.7	15.5	—	24.0	25.5	10.3	35.8
Spain	86	1935.4	298.8	15.4	—	24.0	25.4	10.4	35.8
Netherlands	87	3444.2	530.3	15.4	—	24.0	25.4	10.4	35.8
Italy	88	4590.7	702.4	15.3	—	24.0	25.3	10.5	35.8
Sweden	89	1614.0	246.5	15.3	—	24.0	25.3	10.5	35.8
Norway	90	1104.6	167.8	15.2	—	24.0	25.2	10.6	35.8
Austria	91	1188.3	179.1	15.1	—	24.0	25.1	10.7	35.8
Ecuador	92	219.2	32.9	15.0	—	24.0	25.0	10.8	35.8
Thailand	93	573.9	84.7	14.8	—	24.0	24.8	11.0	35.8
Germany	94	8241.5	1210.8	14.7	—	24.0	24.7	11.1	35.8
France	95	7414.6	1079.9	14.6	—	24.0	24.6	11.2	35.8
Algeria	96	914.4	128.6	14.1	—	24.0	24.1	11.7	35.8
Jordan	97	121.7	16.9	13.9	—	24.0	23.9	11.9	35.8
Fiji	98	51.1	7.0	13.7	—	24.0	23.7	12.1	35.8
Western Samoa	99	8.5	1.1	12.9	—	24.0	22.9	12.9	35.8
Gabon	100	110.3	14.1	12.8	—	24.0	22.8	13.0	35.8
Luxembourg	101	135.5	17.0	12.5	—	24.0	22.5	13.3	35.8
Nigeria	102	1281.6	157.2	12.3	—	24.0	22.3	13.5	35.8
Botswana	103	36.6	4.4	12.0	—	24.0	22.0	13.8	35.8
Bangladesh	104	392.5	47.1	12.0	—	24.0	22.0	13.8	35.8
Suriname	105	67.6	7.8	11.5	—	24.0	21.5	14.3	35.8

	Num.	IMF quota (A)	Net cumulative SDR allocation (B)	C=(B/A)	U.S.-U.K. proposal Option I C+8	Option II	Developing country proposal C+10	Extra increase	Total
		(SDR million)				*(Per cent)*			
Guinea-Bissau	106	10.5	1.2	11.4	—	24.0	21.4	14.4	35.8
Ethiopia	107	98.3	11.2	11.4	—	24.0	21.4	14.4	35.8
Sao Tome and Principe	108	5.5	0.6	10.9	—	24.0	20.9	14.9	35.8
Japan	109	8241.5	891.7	10.8	—	24.0	20.8	15.0	35.8
Comoros	110	6.5	0.7	10.8	—	24.0	20.8	15.0	35.8
Bahamas	111	94.9	10.2	10.7	—	24.0	20.7	15.1	35.8
Grenada	112	8.5	0.9	10.6	—	24.0	20.6	15.2	35.8
Djibouti	113	11.5	1.2	10.4	—	24.0	20.4	15.4	35.8
Romania	114	754.1	76.0	10.1	—	24.0	20.1	15.7	35.8
Dominica	115	6.0	0.6	10.0	—	24.0	20.0	15.8	35.8
United Arab Emirates	116	392.1	38.7	9.9	—	24.0	19.9	15.9	35.8
Papua New Guinea	117	95.3	9.3	9.8	—	24.0	19.8	16.0	35.8
Portugal	118	557.6	53.3	9.6	—	24.0	19.6	16.2	35.8
Solomon Islands	119	7.5	0.7	9.3	—	24.0	19.3	16.5	35.8
Korea, Republic of	120	799.6	72.9	9.1	—	24.0	19.1	16.7	35.8
Cape Verde	121	7.0	0.6	8.6	—	24.0	18.6	17.2	35.8
Bahrain	122	82.8	6.2	7.5	—	24.0	17.5	18.3	35.8
Libya	123	817.6	58.8	7.2	—	24.0	17.2	18.6	35.8
China, People's Rep.	124	3385.2	236.8	7.0	—	24.0	17.0	18.8	35.8
Qatar	125	190.5	12.8	6.7	—	24.0	16.7	19.1	35.8
Seychelles	126	6.0	0.4	6.7	—	24.0	16.7	19.1	35.8
St. Vincent and Grens.	127	6.0	0.4	6.7	—	24.0	16.7	19.1	35.8
St. Lucia	128	11.0	0.7	6.4	—	24.0	16.4	19.4	35.8
Lebanon	129	78.7	4.4	5.6	—	24.0	15.6	20.2	35.8
Maldives	130	5.5	0.3	5.5	—	24.0	15.5	20.3	35.8
Oman	131	119.4	6.3	5.3	—	24.0	15.3	20.5	35.8
Singapore	132	357.6	16.5	4.6	—	24.0	14.6	21.2	35.8
Zimbabwe	133	261.3	10.2	3.9	—	24.0	13.9	21.9	35.8
Saudi Arabia	134	5130.6	195.5	3.8	—	24.0	13.8	22.0	35.8
Kuwait	135	995.2	26.7	2.7	—	24.0	12.7	23.1	35.8
Albania	136	35.3	0.0	0.0	—	24.0	10.0	25.8	35.8
Angola	137	207.3	0.0	0.0	—	24.0	10.0	25.8	35.8
Antigua and Barbuda	138	8.5	0.0	0.0	—	24.0	10.0	25.8	35.8
Armenia	139	67.5	0.0	0.0	—	24.0	10.0	25.8	35.8
Azerbaijan	140	117.0	0.0	0.0	—	24.0	10.0	25.8	35.8
Belarus	141	280.4	0.0	0.0	—	24.0	10.0	25.8	35.8
Belize	142	13.5	0.0	0.0	—	24.0	10.0	25.8	35.8
Bhutan	143	4.5	0.0	0.0	—	24.0	10.0	25.8	35.8
Bulgaria	144	464.9	0.0	0.0	—	24.0	10.0	25.8	35.8
Czech Republic	145	589.6	0.0	0.0	—	24.0	10.0	25.8	35.8
Eritrea	146	11.5	0.0	0.0	—	24.0	10.0	25.8	35.8
Estonia	147	46.5	0.0	0.0	—	24.0	10.0	25.8	35.8
Georgia	148	111.0	0.0	0.0	—	24.0	10.0	25.8	35.8
Hungary	149	754.8	0.0	0.0	—	24.0	10.0	25.8	35.8
Kazakhstan	150	247.5	0.0	0.0	—	24.0	10.0	25.8	35.8
Kiribati	151	4.0	0.0	0.0	—	24.0	10.0	25.8	35.8
Kyrgys Republic	152	64.5	0.0	0.0	—	24.0	10.0	25.8	35.8
Latvia	153	91.5	0.0	0.0	—	24.0	10.0	25.8	35.8
Lithuania	154	103.5	0.0	0.0	—	24.0	10.0	25.8	35.8
Marshall Islands	155	2.5	0.0	0.0	—	24.0	10.0	25.8	35.8
Micronesia	156	3.5	0.0	0.0	—	24.0	10.0	25.8	35.8
Moldova	157	90.0	0.0	0.0	—	24.0	10.0	25.8	35.8
Mongolia	158	37.1	0.0	0.0	—	24.0	10.0	25.8	35.8
Mozambique	159	84.0	0.0	0.0	—	24.0	10.0	25.8	35.8

Table A2 (concluded)

	Num.	IMF quota (A)	Net cumulative SDR allocation (B)	C=(B/A)	U.S.-U.K. proposal Option I C+8	U.S.-U.K. proposal Option II C+10	Developing country proposal Extra increase	Developing country proposal Total
		(SDR million)			*(Per cent)*			
Namibia	160	99.6	0.0	0.0	—	24.0	10.0	25.8	35.8
Poland	161	988.5	0.0	0.0	—	24.0	10.0	25.8	35.8
Russia	162	4313.1	0.0	0.0	—	24.0	10.0	25.8	35.8
San Marino	163	10.0	0.0	0.0	—	24.0	10.0	25.8	35.8
Slovak Republic	164	257.4	0.0	0.0	—	24.0	10.0	25.8	35.8
St. Kitts and Nevis	165	6.5	0.0	0.0	—	24.0	10.0	25.8	35.8
Switzerland	166	2470.4	0.0	0.0	—	24.0	10.0	25.8	35.8
Tajikistan	167	60.0	0.0	0.0	—	24.0	10.0	25.8	35.8
Tonga	168	5.0	0.0	0.0	—	24.0	10.0	25.8	35.8
Turkmenistan	169	48.0	0.0	0.0	—	24.0	10.0	25.8	35.8
Ukraine	170	997.3	0.0	0.0	—	24.0	10.0	25.8	35.8
Uzbekistan	171	199.5	0.0	0.0	—	24.0	10.0	25.8	35.8
Vanuatu	172	12.5	0.0	0.0	—	24.0	10.0	25.8	35.8
All countries		143475.9	21033.1	14.7				
Industrial countries		88425.2	14595.3	16.5				
Developing countries*a*		55050.7	6437.8	11.7				

Source: IMF, *International Financial Statistics*, March 1995.

   a   Seven countries are not included: Haiti, Iraq, Liberia, Somalia, Sudan, Zaire, and Zambia.

THE CASE FOR MULTILATERAL DEBT RELIEF FOR SEVERELY INDEBTED COUNTRIES

Chandra Hardy

Abstract

International financial institutions (IFIs) are becoming the largest creditors of the poorest countries. The severity of the IFI debt burden is a major obstacle to economic recovery in these countries. Their debt-service payments to the World Bank and the IMF have diverted scarce bilateral aid and foreign-exchange receipts from the promotion of economic growth and poverty reduction. There are no legal or financial obstacles to the restructuring of debt owed to IFIs, and the World Bank and the IMF should use their own resources to participate in a comprehensive restructuring of the debt of the poorest countries and to increase the flow of concessional lending.

I. Debt burden

The stock of multilateral debt owed by the developing countries has increased from $98 billion in 1982 to $304 billion in 1992; over the same period, debt-service payments to the multilateral or international financial institutions (IFIs) have increased from $7 billion to $36 billion. The IFIs account for 21 per cent of the total long-term debt of all developing countries; 28 per cent of the debt of the severely indebted low-income countries (SILICs) and 13 per cent of the debt of the severely indebted middle-income countries (SIMICs).

Thirty three countries are classified by the World Bank as severely indebted.[1] This includes 29 (SILICs) out of the 54 low-income countries with a debt/GNP ratio of over 80 per cent and a debt/export ratio of over 220 per cent, and four middle-income countries (SIMICs): Bolivia, Cameroon, Congo and Ivory Coast with similar debt ratios. The stock of IFI debt of SIMICs has increased from $24 billion to $73 billion and debt service has increased from less than $3 billion to $14 billion between 1982 and 1992.[2]

Total SILIC debt at the end of 1993 was $162.3 billion of which 57 per cent was bilateral, 29 per cent was multilateral and 15 per cent private. The stock of

the multilateral debt of SILICs has increased from $11 billion in 1982 to $47 billion in 1993. Most of the borrowing has been concessional, yet debt service to the IFIs has increased from $1 to $3 billion. Since 1988, the share of the IFIs in the debt service paid by SILICs has been more than 40 per cent, and for some African debtors, almost all the debt service paid is to the IFIs.

II. Declining net transfers

The IFIs are lending more and more and are transferring a declining amount of real resources. The net transfers from multilateral creditors to developing countries fell from $13.9 billion in 1982 to $2.4 billion in 1992. "From 1988 to 1992, the net transfers on all debt accounts have been negative $4.6 billion for the SILICs and negative $45 billion for the SIMICs. The net transfers from multilaterals to the SILICs have been low but positive, but net transfers from multilaterals to the SIMICs have been negative since 1987" (Mistry, 1994, p.26).

A declining net transfer is a desirable outcome when countries have reached a stage of development like the Republic of Korea where they no longer need to borrow from the Bank and are in a position to repay their outstanding debt. This is not the case with the highly indebted developing countries which are in need of large positive transfers to promote growth and poverty reduction.

Middle-income developing countries have been very hard hit by large negative net transfers from the IMF since 1986. As long as these countries are able to borrow on the international capital markets, repayments to the IFIs pose less of a burden than to the SILICs which do not have access to private borrowing.

World Bank data indicate that when inflows of foreign investment and grants are taken into account, the net transfers to the SILICs have been declining but positive. However, these numbers often overstate the level of real resource transfers because they do not show the repatriation of profits and dividends, and debt relief is included in the grants. As indicated in the following table, Zambia has received large amounts of external assistance but most of it has gone into servicing debt, mainly to the IFIs. In spite of large gross flows, the net transfer of resources is very limited.

Table 1

NET EXTERNAL FLOWS TO ZAMBIA, 1991-1993

($ million)

	1991	1992	1993
Commodity aid	76	246	90
Balance-of-payments support			
World Bank	202	165	144
Other sources	264	326	155
Project loans	244	191	234
Total external flows	786	928	623
Debt relief	1158	551	359
Debt service	-1841	-926	-710
Net transfers	103	553	272

Source: SASDA, 1994.

III. Debt, adjustment and recovery

Most of the severely indebted countries are in sub-Saharan Africa (SSA) and the build-up of IFI debt has not helped to bring about their economic recovery. Between 1980 and 1992, IFI debt to SSA increased by $43 billion but over this period, the GNP of the region fell by $24 billion and exports were lower by nearly $3 billion. Evaluations by both Fund and Bank staff indicate that the achievements of the structural adjustment programmes in low-income countries have been minimal. The build-up in lending did not achieve the desired results and the borrowers should not have to bear the entire burden of over-optimistic projections and exogenous shocks.[3]

SSA is more heavily indebted and further away from economic recovery than it was in 1980. The population has grown by 50 per cent and the economic and social infrastructure is in an extreme state of disrepair. The failure to write off debts which were unsustainable in 1980 has created more debt and caused enormous loss in life and well-being in the poorest countries. Over the past decade, the region has experienced a decline in import volumes at 2-3 per cent per annum, a deterioration in the terms of trade at 4 per cent per annum, a decline in per capita income of 1 per cent per annum, and the debt indicators have worsened. From 1982 to 1992, the debt/GNP ratio increased from 49 per cent to 105 per cent; the debt/exports ratio increased from 266 per cent to 413 per cent and the share of debt paid to total exports fell from 33 per cent to 21 per cent.

IV. The provision of debt relief

Over the past decade, bilateral creditors have taken a number of measures to provide debt relief to the poorest and heavily indebted countries. They have written down their own debt and accepted delays in payment to enable borrowers to service debts to the IFIs. They have progressively eased the terms of rescheduling at the Paris Club (Venice, Houston, Toronto, Trinidad and enhanced Toronto). They have provided concessional funds to the IFIs to refinance their non-concessional debt. They have provided extraordinary financing for Support Groups for Guyana, Cameroon, Zambia and Peru, and the Nordic countries have provided concessional resources to pay off the principal and interest on IFI debt. Despite all of this, both the stock of debt and the debt service burden of severely indebted low and middle-income countries have increased.

The debt obligations to multilateral creditors have not been formally rescheduled or reduced. The IFI's have dealt with the problem of their growing claims by refinancing their non-concessional debt using an ingenious variety of methods and by making new loans on concessional terms. However, the IFIs have not used their own resources for the refinancing. The full cost of the refinancing and the increase in net IFI flows to severely indebted countries have been met by donor Governments.

V. Obligations to the IMF

Debt owed by developing countries to the IMF increased by 60 per cent between 1982 and 1992. The bulk of the lending was to the SIMICs whose debt to the IMF quadrupled over the period, while the debt of the SILICs rose by 41 per cent. Until 1988, debtor countries used their own reserves or bridging loans from Central or commercial banks to clear their arrears to the Fund. The IMF would then make a loan to enable the country to repay the bridging loan. In April 1988, the first donor Support Group was formed to help Guyana clear its arrears to the IMF.

Guyana was declared ineligible for IMF credit in 1985 because of the build-up of arrears, and by 1988 its total debt had grown to $1.8 billion, including $1.0 billion in arrears; this was more than six times the level of exports and the debt service ratio was 89 per cent. In 1988, the Bank and the Fund began the process of helping Guyana to clear these arrears. The chairman of the Support Group who was the Executive Director for Canada at the IMF together with Bank and Fund staff, visited the capitals of the major donor countries to put together a financing package of $1.9 billion including $1.2 billion eligible for debt rescheduling at the Paris Club.

The financing package was not finalized in 1989, but to keep the effort alive, Guyana was required to undertake adjustment measures without any external assistance from the IFIs. In June 1990, Guyana cleared its arrears to the Fund using a bridging loan from a commercial bank, and the Fund made loans to Guyana totalling SDR 131 million which was used to repay the bridging loan. Arrears to the World Bank of $55.3 million were also cleared and the Bank made an IDA credit of SDR 59.8 million. Likewise, arrears to the Caribbean Development Bank (CDB) of $30 million were cleared and the CDB made a concessional loan of $42 million.[4] The refinancing of these arrears with concessional loans from the IFIs and bilateral assistance did not reduce Guyana's debt burden. At the end of 1992, the country's total debt was $1.9 billion which was more than nine times the level of exports.

The clearance of these arrears required giving Guyana extended access to the Fund's resources and placed a large claim on donor funds. To minimize these difficulties, the Fund came up in April 1991 with the Rights Accumulation Programme (RAP) which was funded out of the General Resources. Under this programme, the IMF provides a limited amount of debt forgiveness. Arrears to the Fund are frozen for three-four years during which time, the borrowers are required to pay off the interest charges in arrears, meet current debt service payments and implement a stabilization programme without assistance from the Fund.

The conditionality of "rights" programmes is stringent. The IMF sets quarterly financing targets for the Government by specifying ceilings on reserve money creation, domestic credit expansion and short-term external borrowing. Successful attainment of these targets allows the Government to accumulate rights with which to redeem outstanding IMF credits. Disbursements are made only when sufficient rights have been accumulated to repay a bridging loan contracted to clear the arrears.[5] Interest charges account for 30 per cent of the arrears to the Fund and donor support is needed to enable countries to clear these arrears and to meet debt service payments to the IMF during a three-four year period of negative transfers.

Zambia was the first country to use a RAP to clear arrears to the Fund. In 1991, Zambia used aid to clear $125 million in arrears to the IMF, and it used aid ($120 million) and a Bank of England bridging loan of $200 million to clear arrears to the World Bank. However, Zambia failed to attain many of the IMF targets and World Bank conditions, and its RAP programme was suspended in September 1991. Zambia then had to use a commercial bank loan of $51 million to clear arrears and resume the programme in 1992. The RAP period has been extended and Zambia is still trying to implement the programme. As of end 1993, the country's total debt was $6.8 billion, almost 2.5 times its GDP and 6 times its exports.

Of the 12 countries in arrears to the IMF in 1993, only three have so far used the RAP approach: Peru, Zambia and Sierra Leone. But only Peru has succeeded in clearing its arrears with the Fund. Three countries have received help from Donor Support groups - Guyana, Cambodia and Honduras. Panama and Viet Nam used their own reserves and bridging loans to clear arrears. Liberia, Somalia, Sudan and Zaïre have arrears amounting to 400-700 per cent of their quotas and are beyond refinancing by the IMF since the IMF could not provide access to its resources to this extent.

VI. Obligations to the World Bank

Since 1988, some of the repayments on IDA credits have been used to assist eligible SILICs to repay the interest on earlier IBRD loans. This is known as the "fifth dimension" of the Special Assistance Programme for Africa. The total amount allocated under the programme during 1988-1992 was more than $520 million. In addition, Finland, Norway and Sweden provided aid to refinance both the principal and interest payments on IBRD loans.

In 1989 the Bank allocated $100 million out of its net income to establish the Debt Reduction Facility to enable IDA countries to buy back their commercial debt at a discount, and in 1994, another $100 million out of net income was added to the Facility. The Bank has also made loans (to the Philippines and Uruguay) which could be used to buy back commercial bank debt, and it has ensured that IDA flows to countries implementing structural adjustment programmes are sufficient to cover debt service to the Bank.

In May 1991, the Bank introduced its version of the RAP, called "Additional Support for Workout Programmes in Countries with Protracted Arrears". Eligible countries accumulate rights to disbursements during a performance period and the disbursements are made when the arrears have been cleared. For Peru the Bank's performance period was the same as the Fund's, but it was shorter for Zambia and Sierra Leone because the amounts in arrears were smaller.

VII. Reliance on bilateral support

The arrears to the Bank and the Fund have so far been cleared using bilateral aid. During 1990-1991, Nicaragua, Panama, Sierra Leone and Zambia cleared their arrears to the World Bank with the help of donors and bridging loans. In 1993, Peru cleared its arrears to the IMF using funds from the United States Treasury and Japan's Eximbank as well as $10 million of its own funds. The IMF then made a loan to Peru which was used to clear arrears to the Bank, and disbursements from the World Bank were used to repay the United States and Japan.

The external financing needed from donors has been consider-able. The Support Group for Peru led by Japan provided $422 million in 1991 and $500 million in 1992. Zambia's programme required bilateral support totalling $750 million a year in 1991 and 1992. "Despite this support, however, a durable solution to the SILIC debt problem has not been reached" (World Bank, 1994a, p.iii). Most SILICs are unable to meet their debt-service obligations and arrears continue to build-up.

Other indicators of the severity of the problem are:

- The need for repeated debt rescheduling. The number of negotiations between African Governments and creditor agencies has been estimated at nearly 8,000 between 1980 and 1992 (Killick, 1993).

- Widespread recognition by the financial markets that the debt will never be repaid. This is reflected in the heavy discounting of the private debt of low-income countries.

- Recognition that the Paris Club approach only offers temporary relief and increases the size of the debt, leading to calls by several donors for writing off the debt of the poorest countries.

- Estimates by the World Bank that the application of the most concessional rescheduling terms being offered (enhanced Toronto terms) to all low-income borrowers would still leave the majority of SILICs with an unmanageable debt burden.

- The steady increase in arrears to the Bank and the Fund. Arrears to the IMF have risen from SDR 30 million in 1982 to SDR 3.0 billion in 1993, and arrears to the World Bank were $2.5 billion in 1993 despite considerable refinancing of IBRD obligations.

VIII. Liquidity or solvency problem?

In its analysis of the SILIC debt problem, the World Bank examines whether existing debt-servicing obligations pose a liquidity constraint or a solvency problem. The conclusion reached is that the SILICs do not have a liquidity problem because they receive substantial grants. The Bank report does note, however, that these grants have to be considered a permanent source of income to the country if it is to be concluded that the present level of debt servicing is sustainable.

The SILICs have a solvency problem, according to the Bank, since debt service ratios of 15 per cent are high and debt/export ratios of over 200 per cent are not sustainable. The debt burden of most of the severely indebted countries exceed these ratios. The report concludes that these countries are not likely to grow out of the problem. Therefore, the large debt overhang needs to be eliminated and debt reduction, the report states, provides the most direct means to eliminate the overhang. However, the Bank's view is that reducing the bilateral debt overhang (which accounts for about 60 per cent of the debt stock of the SILICs) and ensuring adequate new flows of grants must be the central element of the debt strategy.[6]

IX. Severity of the IFI debt burden

There are currently 12 SILICs with multilateral debt/exports ratios of over 150 per cent, Burundi, Guinea-Bissau, Nicaragua, Sao Tome & Principe, Somalia, Sudan, Tanzania, Uganda, Guyana, Liberia, Rwanda and Zambia, and in all but two of these countries IFI debt service exceeds exports plus grants.

The IFIs account for almost 30 per cent of the debt of the SILICs and their share will continue to grow in the 1990s as the loans made in the 1980s begin to fall due and most bilateral creditors have been making grants and writing off their loans to low-income countries.

Table 2

SILIC DEBT BY CREDITOR, 1993

	$billion	Per cent of total
Bilateral	91.8	57
Multilateral	46.7	29
of which		
IDA	19.4	
IBRD	6.8	
IMF	5.8	
Private	23.7	15
Total	*162.3*	*100*

Source: World Bank, Debtor Reporting System

The major burden of IFI debt, however, is its claim on the debt service paid by the poorest countries. In 1992, 46 per cent of the debt service paid went to private creditors, 40 per cent to the IFIs, and only 14 per cent to bilateral creditors. However, the IFIs received 84 per cent of the debt service due, private creditors received 69 per cent and the bilateral creditors received 14 per cent. In 1993, the share of the IFIs in the debt service paid jumped to 49 per cent and the share of private creditors fell to 23 per cent.

The share of the IFIs in the debt service paid will remain large over the coming decade (table 3) since the share of private debt is declining and the Paris Club is expected to continue to provide relief on bilateral debt.

Table 3

PROJECTIONS FOR SILIC DEBT SERVICE, 1994-2003
($ billion)

	Bilateral	Multilateral	Private	Total
1994	10.26	3.58	2.58	16.42
1995	10.00	3.67	2.21	15.88
1996	9.24	3.78	1.89	14.91
1997	8.23	3.89	1.50	13.62
1998	7.53	3.75	1.33	12.61
1999	7.25	3.46	1.17	11.88
2000	5.88	3.16	0.95	9.99
2001	4.64	2.95	0.87	8.46
2002	3.90	2.72	0.83	7.45
2003	3.55	2.60	0.79	6.94

Source: World Bank, Debtor Reporting System

The principal arguments in favour of IFI debt relief are:

(1) The use of bilateral assistance to refinance and service IFI debt is not an effective use of donor funds.

Bilateral creditors have to cancel large stocks of their own debt and provide concessional resources to the IFIs for debt relief. But lending by the IFIs has increased the debt and debt-service burden without bringing about an improvement in the economic situation of the debtor countries, and the stabilization and adjustment programmes have had harsh social costs. Another consideration is that a disproportionate share of donor funds goes directly to the multilateral creditors and is used for balance-of-payments support and debt relief. This leaves next to nothing for other priorities of development assistance such as support for the social sectors, women and the environment.

(2)   The need to clear arrears and keep current on debt service to IFIs distorts the pattern of development financing.

Despite all the exhortation about ownership, the budget and economic policies are determined by the Bank and the Fund. This has resulted in a situation where the only development policy many low-income borrowers can pursue is the one dictated and micro-managed by the IFIs. This has not helped them to find a way out of the present crisis.

(3)   The need for quick disbursing loans determines the size and composition of IFI lending programmes.

Since the early 1980s, the policies of the Bank and the Fund have focused on issues of short-term stabilization rather than long-term structural adjustment and balanced growth, and the amount of balance-of-payments support provided is determined by the need to avoid a build-up in arrears. Project loans which disburse over a longer period (up to eight years) and require more technical, managerial and supervisory ability have given way to sector and policy-based lending. Disbursements on projects to rehabilitate roads, schools and factories would not be large enough or fast enough to ensure positive net flows to the country.

(4)   Reducing the stock of the debt of all creditors would free resources for growth and poverty alleviation.

The external capital requirements of SSA were estimated at roughly $30 billion per annum for the period 1991-2000. Under existing arrangements, half of these inflows would go to debt servicing. Therefore, they would not be available for economic development. At the projected level of imports, the region could expect to regain in 2000 the per capita income of 1980 (IMF, 1992).

The arguments against the provision of IFI debt relief fall into two categories - those affecting the debtor countries and those affecting the financial standing of the World Bank and the IMF. With regard to the debtor countries, the arguments have been that

SSA has received substantial net transfers in recent years; that addressing the debt issue in isolation will not offer lasting solutions; that there are only 14 African countries with a significant multilateral debt problem; and that the Bank has taken a number of measures to reduce this burden.

However, the issue is not being addressed in isolation. The solution being sought is to attain a sustainable debt burden which is a necessary condition for economic recovery. The relevant consideration is not the low share of non-concessional IFI debt to total SILIC debt, or the increasing concessionality of IFI flows to SILICs but the fact that debt servicing exceeds 20 per cent of export earnings for the majority of the SILICS, and the Bank and the Fund take up 40 per cent or more of the debt service paid.

It is also argued that debt relief would not necessarily generate additional resources to the debtor countries. Since the major reason for proposing comprehensive debt reduction is to increase the net resource transfer, it would be counter-productive for creditors to agree to the proposal and then provide the relief in such a way that there is no increase in net transfers. Such an outcome is possible when there is a divergence of views between Treasury and aid agency officials in the creditor countries. For this reason, close attention will need to be given to the modalities of providing the debt relief.

The moral-hazard or free-rider problem is another objection. Across-the-board debt relief, it is argued, would reward the countries which are unwilling to accept conditionality. But the number of countries which have been unwilling or unable to adopt structural adjustment programmes have been far fewer than those which have been implementing Bank/Fund programmes for over a decade. Of the eight countries currently in arrears to the Bank (Syria, Liberia, Iraq, Congo, Zaïre, Sudan, Federal Republic of Yugoslavia, and Bosnia-Herzegovina), only three are not discussing structural adjustment loans and five are hampered by internal and external conflicts.

The concern about whether debt relief should be provided on a case-by-case basis or across-the-board is also a question of the modalities. After the eligibility criteria are agreed upon, the provision of debt relief should be across-the-board for all severely indebted borrowers. The precedent for the efficacy of this approach is the 1970 rescheduling of all of Indonesia's debt and the 1953 rescheduling of all of Germany's pre- and post-war debts. The determination of the appropriate level of new flows would then be done on a case-by-case basis for borrowers willing to undertake economic recovery programmes.

X. Debt relief from the World Bank

The view of the World Bank is that the provision of debt relief would erode its preferred status as a borrower and raise the cost of funds. "The policy of non-rescheduling and non write offs is an essential element in mobilizing finance from capital markets on the best possible terms. For instance, the policy is a factor in the triple A rating" (World Bank 1994a, p. 44). However, this is a considerable overstatement.

The preferred-creditor status of the World Bank is not a legal obligation of the borrowers. As noted by the Associate General Counsel of the World Bank, "there is no specific commitment to preferred-creditor treatment in the Articles of Agreement or loan agreement" (Adams, 1994, p.29). The preferred-creditor status is simply a convention or courtesy granted by creditor Governments which are willing to subordinate their debt to those of the IFIs and to provide resources to enable the Bank to maintain a positive cash flow to the highly indebted countries.

Taxpayers in the donor countries pay for the Bank's preferred creditor status, and without this support the various techniques used by the Bank and the Fund to refinance their non-concessional debt would not function. A 1992 investigation by the Auditor General of Canada noted that borrowers have been supported "through bilateral and multilateral programmes to enable them to service their debts to the World Bank and ...one must ask whether these flows can be maintained indefinitely.[7]

The preferred-creditor status is not given voluntarily by the borrowing countries to the Bank and the Fund, but rather under duress. By informal agreement among the creditors, borrowers are confronted with a total suspension of official loans and debt relief if they do not service IFI debts and accept a Bank/Fund stabilization and adjustment programme.

The provision of debt relief would not raise the borrowing costs of the World Bank for several reasons:

(i)   The perception of weakness in the Bank's portfolio is more likely to arise out of evaluations such as the Wapenhans report (World Bank, 1992) - which found over one-third of the Bank's $140 billion in projects to be failing - than on the need to provide debt relief under exceptional circumstances to borrowers which can never repay the debt.

(ii)   The triple-A rating of the Bank which determines its cost of borrowing does not depend on the convention of the preferred creditor status but on the binding legal obligation of the members to provide callable capital if needed to pay the bondholders.

The Caribbean Development Bank, which has a capital stock of $650 million (or less than half of one per cent of the World Bank's subscribed capital of $170 billion) and a much more concentrated loan portfolio, also has a triple-A rating. And the African Development Bank with a capital stock of $21 billion and more than half of its borrowers in arrears, also has a triple-A rating. This suggests that as long as its financial ratios remain within prudent limits and the borrowing stays within the level of guarantees of the major shareholders the World Bank will maintain its high credit rating.

(iii)   The World Bank is one of the world's largest borrowers and its financial condition is exceptionally strong. This enables the Bank to choose when and where to borrow to lower costs.[8]

The Bank maintains a liquid asset portfolio of $20 billion. The primary reason for holding so much liquidity "is to ensure flexibility in its borrowing decisions should borrowing be adversely affected by temporary conditions in the capital markets" (World Bank, 1994b, p.168). In addition, the Bank has numerous options at its disposal to minimize the cost of borrowed funds including the use of short-term and variable-rate instruments, currency swaps, prepayments, repurchases and the refinancing of higher-cost borrowing.

In 1993, the Bank borrowed $12.2 billion in twelve currencies and in as many countries. The average maturity of the medium- and long-term debt was 7.4 years at an average cost of 5.03 per cent p.a.. The Bank faces no currency or interest-rate risks on its debt since both are passed on to its borrowers.

The Bank estimates that the loss of the preferred-creditor status could lead to an increase of between 10 and 50 basis points in the cost of funds (World Bank, 1994a). If the larger figure is used, the estimated increase in borrowing cost would be $500 million for all IBRD borrowers. This is not a small sum, but it would be spread over a large number of borrowers (66) which are better able to pay the higher rate and/or choose not to borrow from the Bank.

The World Bank is legally authorized to make changes in its loan agreements to adapt to changing circumstances both at the project level and at the country level. The Articles of Agreement contain two provisions that specifically address the rescheduling of loan terms. Article IV, Section 4 provides:

> If a member suffers from an acute exchange stringency, so that the service of any loan contracted by that member cannot be provided in the stipulated manner, the member may apply to the Bank for a relaxation of the conditions of repayment. If the Bank is satisfied that some relaxation is in the interests of the particular member and of the operations of the Bank and of its members as a whole, it may take action under either, or both, of the following paragraphs with respect to the whole, or part, of the annual service:
>
> (i) The Bank may, in its discretion accept service payments in the members own currency for a period not to exceed three years.
>
> (ii) The Bank may modify the terms of amortization or extend the life of the loan, or both.

The World Bank has on numerous occasions agreed to a rescheduling of its loans on project grounds, but only in a few cases (Haiti, India, Bangladesh) has the Bank agreed to reschedule loan maturities on the grounds of undue hardship arising from an acute scarcity of foreign exchange suffered by the borrowing country. In making adjustments to the repayment of its loans, the Bank has relied on its general powers and responded in the context of an ongoing dialogue with the borrowing country rather than on any particular provision of the Articles of Agreement. However, it is clear that the Articles of Agreement give the borrowers the right to request a restructuring of the debt in situations of extreme hardship and empower the Bank to respond to such requests.

The provision of debt relief by the Bank would involve the restructuring of the IBRD debt of the severely indebted countries on IDA terms and the cancellation of interest in arrears. The cost could be more than adequately covered by a small part of the provisions and reserves, totalling $18.0 billion in 1994 which were accumulated to protect the operations of the institution from the consequences of non-payment. Moreover, if the debt is restructured as it falls due, the impact on the Bank's key financial indicators would be negligible.

XI. Debt relief from the IMF

The IMF does not borrow on the international capital markets to make its loans. The bulk of its funds come from the paid-in subscriptions of its member countries. Each country makes a subscription to the General Resources account equal to its assigned quota, and the IMF uses these resources to make short-term balance-of-payments loans at commercial interest rates. Total quotas in the Fund currently amount to SDR 145 billion or $200 billion.

The IMF's holdings of gold result from the fact that, in accordance with the Fund's Articles of Agreement, in 1944 each member country paid in 25 per cent of its quota in gold and 75 per cent in its own currency. Paid-in subscriptions to the IMF are counted as part of a member country's reserves and the first 25 per cent (reserve tranche) is payable on demand. Drawings in the upper credit tranches are conditional.

The IMF argues that the provision of debt relief would lead to a perception that the resources in the General Account which are counted as assets by its members are not risk-free. This argument carries less weight than that of the World Bank which is concerned about the assessment of its creditworthiness by a large number of bondholders and money managers. In the case of the IMF, the riskiness of its resources will be assessed by highly knowledgeable Governors of Central Banks, and subscriptions to the IMF are only a small part of a country's reserves.

The Second Amendment of the Articles of Agreement of the IMF (adopted in 1976) gave the Fund the ability to respond flexibly to the needs of its members in response to major disruptions in international trade and payments. Included in the amendments were the authority to reduce the Fund's holdings of gold and to make adjustments to its financial operations and transactions. This authority was used by the IMF to establish the Trust Fund to make longer-term, concessional loans to the poorest countries.

The Trust Fund was financed with the profits from the sale of 25 million ounces of gold between 1976 and 1980. The sales of gold financed a Trust Fund of SDR 3 billion which made loans to 62 low-income countries with maturities of 10 years including 5.5 years grace and an interest rate of 0.5 per cent. The Second Amendment of the Articles of Agreement also gave the IMF the authority to defer repayment of Trust Fund loans or to suspend all obligations to repay if the scheduled debt service caused undue hardship.

Trust Fund operations were halted in 1980 and all repayments were returned to the General Resources account.

The Structural Adjustment Facility (SAF) which the IMF established in 1986 had the same purpose as the Trust Fund, namely to make concessional loans to the same 62 low-income countries which were eligible for Trust Fund loans, but the funds available were inadequate. To supplement the SAF, the IMF established in 1989, the Enhanced Structural Adjustment Facility (ESAF). These two facilities enabled the Fund to extend loans for up to 10 years with 5.5 years grace at concessional interest rates (0.5 per cent). Funds under these facilities have been disbursed slowly because of reductions in access limits and the unwillingness or inability of borrowers to adhere to IMF targets. SAF and ESAF have refinanced only 40 per cent of the repayments of low-income countries of non-concessional IMF debt (Mistry, 1994, p.49).

The SAF was funded using the reflows from Trust Fund loans, and ESAF was funded from Trust Fund reflows and the contributions from 17 industrial countries. The IMF could thus provide debt relief on SAF and ESAF loans without compromising the quality of its members' reserve assets. This would still leave borrowers with the burden of the higher-cost debt owed to the IMF. At the end of February 1993, non-concessional IMF loans to low-income countries amounted to $6.2 billion, of which $2.1 billion were to SILICs.

The United States and the Scandanavian countries suggested further gold sales to fund the SAF and ESAF. Instead, the IMF Board agreed to set aside 3 million ounces of gold (valued at roughly SDR 1 billion) as a reserve against non-repayment and indicated that if the RAP approach did not succeed in eliminating arrears to the Fund this reserve would be used to cover overdue commitments. However, no procedures have been put in place as yet to make this effective.

XII. Gold sales

The funds for ESAF will be exhausted during 1994-1995. A broad consensus has emerged on the need for a much enlarged concessional facility in the IMF, funded from its own resources. Several proposals have been made for the IMF to sell 10-15 per cent of its holdings of gold (100 million ounces

valued today at $375 per ounce) to write off its non-concessional debt and increase its lending to the poorest countries. IMF staff have responded that the financial stability of the institution rests on its gold holdings. Even if this were the case, it is difficult to see how this stability is undermined by the sale of 10 per cent of this stock which is officially valued by the IMF at $42 per ounce.

The Second Amendment of the Articles of Agreement eliminated gold from the operations of the Fund. The part of the quota that used to be payable in gold is now paid in SDRs or currencies approved by the IMF. During 1976-1980, the IMF disposed of one-third (50 million ounces) of its gold holdings [9] without impairing its financial stability. Since 1980 the Fund has not used gold in any of its operations.

A second argument used is that the price of gold is depressed. The price of gold has been under $400 per ounce for the past decade but the profit to the IMF from the sale of gold at today's prices would still be substantial. In 1976 and 1977, gold was sold for $148-155 per ounce. The case against gold sales must be made on something other than speculation about the price of gold.

XIII. SDR allocation

Proposals have also been made for a special allocation of SDRs for the purpose of writing off debt to the IMF. The response has been that according to the present rules, allocations would be according to the size of a country's quota and use of the allocations would be at market rates of interest. But these rules can be changed by agreement among the members, and creditor countries could provide their allocations as grants to those in need and forego the earning of market interest rates on a created asset.

The main argument against a special SDR allocation has usually been the fear that the creation of liquidity would create pressures leading to a resumption of world inflation. However, the probability that enhancing the liquidity position of the world's poorest countries would set off a spiral of world inflation seems to be small. Inflation in the industrial countries is much more a result of longer-term structural factors than excess demand, and increased imports from the low-income countries would increase demand marginally, if at all, without necessarily contributing to inflationary pressures in the world economy given current rates of unemployment in the industrial countries.

The IMF has both the resources and the legal authority to provide debt relief to the poorest countries. The total assets of the Fund amount to over SDR 150 billion including SDR 139 billion in subscriptions, borrowing of SDR 3.4 billion and gold (valued at the official price of SDR 35 per ounce) amounting to SDR 3.6 billion. In 1993, the Fund's liquidity (i.e. the pool of usable currencies) totalled SDR 52.2 billion, an increase of over SDR 30 billion over the previous year because of the 1992 quota increase, and the use of the Fund's resources amounted to SDR 24.6 billion. Since the mid-1980s, the IMF has also taken measures to build up its reserves against non-payment.

Article V, Section 7(g) of the Articles of Agreement of the IMF was substantially revised under the Second Amendment. As in the World Bank, members have the right to apply for an extension of the due date of a loan, and the Board of Directors of the Fund can, with a 70 per cent majority, extend the due date beyond 10 years.

XIV. Benefits to the IFIs of debt relief

The provision of comprehensive debt relief would not only benefit the severely indebted countries but would also improve the balance sheets and operational policies of the Bank and the Fund. The present methods of refinancing their non-concessional debt masks the weakness in their loan portfolios. Currently, the Bank shows only eight countries, and the IMF ten countries, with arrears of over six months, but the IFI debts of many countries would not be serviced if the creditor countries did not provide the resources to ensure repayment.[10]

The low level of arrears also masks the failure of the IMF/World Bank sponsored adjustment programmes to bring about recovery and improve the creditworthiness of the debtor countries. It leads to a situation in which the policy dialogue is totally dominated by the need to avoid the build-up of IFI arrears, and the size of policy-based lending is not determined by any objective criteria of absorptive capacity or income-generation potential.

Finally, the present methods do not provide a lasting solution to reducing the debt burden. The refinancing of IFI debt, even on concessional terms, simply postpones the problem. Given the rising share of the IFIs in the total debt and debt service, and the increasing number of countries that accumulate arrears, the Bank and the Fund will be required to take the leadership in finding a durable solution to the problem.

XV. Conclusion

Reports prepared by the IMF (1994) and the World Bank IMF (1994a) confirm the severity of the debt problem of the poorest countries. The World Bank identifies 29 severely indebted low-income countries and four severely indebted middle-income countries, and the IMF identifies 34 low-income rescheduling countries. Both studies indicate that the share of the debt owed to IFIs is increasing, and in many cases it is unsustainably large. The share of the IFIs in the debt of low-income rescheduling countries increased from 25 per cent in 1980 to about 44 per cent in 1991. 20 out of the 29 SILICs had IFI debt in excess of 100 per cent of exports and eight had IFI debt in excess of 200 per cent of exports.

The World Bank study recognizes that the debt overhang and debt service is a constraint on the long-term development of the severely indebted countries and recommends a write-off of the bilateral debt. However, the IFIs are becoming the main creditors to these countries, and the projected debt service to the IFIs over the coming decade is the major obstacle to their economic recovery.

In a recent paper prepared jointly by the staff of the Bank and the Fund for the Executive Directors, a stylized framework is used to project the future debt service to the IFIs for 34 out of 41 countries characterized as heavily indebted poor countries (IMF/World Bank, 1995). The explicit assumptions behind the projections pertain to export growth and increased lending on concessional terms by the IFIs over the period 1995-2014. The implicit assumptions about the provision of debt relief by other creditors and the terms of non-IFI borrowing are not indicated in the paper.

Under scenario I, exports (defined as goods, services and workers remittances) grow at 3 per cent per annum in dollar terms, but 18 of the 34 countries still show an IFI-debt-service ratio of over 10 per cent. Under scenario II, the rate of growth of exports after 1997 doubles to 6 per cent per annum in nominal terms, and disbursements from the IFIs on concessional terms are constant in real terms, but 14 of the 34 countries still show an IFI-debt-service ratio of over 10 per cent. The paper concludes that these countries need to mobilize resources on even more concessional terms.

Under scenario III, the same assumptions are made as under scenario II, but after 1998 new lending does not come from IFIs but in the form of bilateral grants; this brings down the IFI-debt-service ratio. The conclusion of the study that the IFI debt burden is manageable is based solely on projections which show the IFI-debt-service ratio declining for most of the 34 countries to below 10 per cent. However, the methodological basis of the study is deeply flawed.

The determination of the severity of the IFI debt burden cannot be based solely on the share of the IFIs in the debt service. The IFI debt presents a problem for borrowers if the payment of debt service has a negative impact on their economic development. The diversion of scarce, untied, balance-of-payments assistance to debt servicing, mainly to the Bank and the Fund, must be considered against per capita incomes which have been declining for two decades and which - under optimistic assumptions - can be expected to regain their 1980 level in 2000. The borrowers need higher levels of imports to promote recovery and alleviate poverty, and the payment of 20 per cent of their considerably reduced export earnings in debt service causes undue hardship.

The countries excluded from the projections are Angola, Congo, Liberia, Somalia, Sudan, Zaïre and Zambia. These countries have a total population of 100 million, a total debt of $54 billion and multilateral debt accounting for 20 per cent of the total debt. Their IFI debt problem cannot be ignored indefinitely and special arrangements cannot be made for these countries which exclude the other heavily indebted countries.

The joint Bank/Fund study should be extended so as to include individual projections for each of the 41 heavily indebted countries. These projections should take due account of the requirements for growth and the fiscal impact of the debt service. They should assess:

- the level of resource transfers needed for adequate growth of per capita incomes and poverty reduction;

- the level of investment needed to sustain export growth at 6 per cent per annum in dollar terms;

- the trends in the terms of trade and the capacity to import (if the terms of trade deteriorate, countries have to allocate more export earnings to essential imports, 29 January 1996leaving less for debt servicing);

- the impact of shocks which would undoubtedly interrupt the growth of exports and capital inflows.

The projected level of concessional disbursements from the IFIs should be put in the context of the required levels of funding for the IDA and ESAF replenishment. The Bank/Fund study shows concessional disbursements from the IFIs for 34 countries increasing from $6 billion in 1994 to $8 billion in 2004 and $10 billion in 2014, but no assessment is made as to whether sufficient finance will in fact be available.

To further the discussion of the IFI debt burden of the poorest countries, developing countries should also request information from the Bank and the Fund regarding:

(i) the factors influencing previous reschedulings of IFI debt on the grounds of exchange stringency and undue hardship;

(ii) the details about IMF gold sales between 1976 and 1980; and

(iii) the returns to the IMF of its gold holdings.

The Bank and the Fund have shown considerable ingenuity in coming up with measures to refinance their debt and prevent the build-up of arrears. The technique of using new money to pay off old debts is not new but it has a limited life. The method breaks down when the sources of new money dry up.

In May 1994 the Swedish and Swiss Governments hosted a seminar on the external debt situation of the SILICs. Several participants referred to the growing lack of support among officials and non-governmental organizations for increased contributions to the concessional windows of the IFIs. Many donors have called for IFI debt relief and a reconsideration of the policy of IFIs not to reschedule or forgive debt.

The existing stock of debt of the poorest countries cannot be repaid. The size of the debt and debt service claims by the IFIs distort the pattern of development financing and are not sustainable. Therefore, the Fund and the Bank should be part of a comprehensive restructuring of these countries' debt, using their own funds for this purpose. The present practice of using bilateral aid to service IFI debt is both inequitable and inefficient. Bilateral aid could be better utilized to promote more lasting development in the borrowing countries, and the IFIs could better manage their finances through the use of their own resources.

The provision of debt relief by the Fund and the Bank would require a waiver of the interest charges in arrears, and the remaining IBRD/IMF non-concessional debt to be written off or converted into IDA terms. The restructuring of part of the SILIC debt outstanding to the Bank (about $7 billion) and to the Fund ($6 billion) can be accommodated without any adverse consequences to their financial standing. The Fund's assets exceed $200 billion and the authorized capital of the Bank is $184 billion. Both institutions have liquid assets in excess of $20 billion which would ensure no interruption in their operations, and ample reserves to cushion debt reduction. The World Bank is such a large force in the capital markets that it is unlikely to suffer any increase in its borrowing cost. Both institutions should also use their own resources to enlarge their concessional lending to the poorest countries.

The IMF has the authority to sell gold and re-establish the Trust Fund to provide grants to severely indebted countries to retire debts to the IMF. There are no overwhelming technical arguments against the sales of gold or a special allocation of SDRs. Technical constraints can be removed if there is the political will to do so. There appears to be more of a consensus among the major shareholders on the sales of gold than on an allocation of SDRs but this is a decision which has to be made by the Board of Directors of the IMF.

Finally, the Articles of Agreement give the legal authority to the World Bank and the IMF to restructure their loans to the poorest countries on the grounds of acute foreign exchange stringency and undue hardship. There is little argument that both conditions are met.

Notes

1   The IMF and the World Bank do not use the same classification of severely indebted countries. The IMF focuses on 34 low-income rescheduling countries, and the World Bank on 29 severely indebted low-income countries (SILICs) - of which only 21 fall into the IMF grouping - and four severely indebted middle-income countries (SIMICs).

2   The IFI debt is also a burden for a large number of moderately indebted low- and middle-income countries. A better measure of the IFI debt burden is the number of countries with more than 40 per cent of their debt service going to the IFIs, which was 43 in 1991 (Martin, 1993). However, this paper uses the World Bank's grouping for which data are more readily available.

3   Several commentators have criticized the tendency for IMF/World Bank projections to understate the resource gap which causes frequent breakdowns in adjustment programmes and the underfunding of capital investment.

4   Lending packages do not usually require that borrowers clear the arrears with all multilateral institutions as in the case of Guyana. For this reason, debts to the Bank and the Fund have been paid elsewhere at the expense of other multilateral institutions, including the African Development Bank.

5   The Fund has eliminated special charges on countries in arrears since this worsened the problem and was not a deterrent to the accumulation of arrears.

6   E. Jaycox, Vice-President, Africa Region, remarks to the Geneva seminar, May 1994.

7   Report of the Auditor-General of Canada to the House of Commons 1992, p.286.

8   The Bank's total authorized capital is $184 billion and it can sustain a level of lending of $30 billion a year (almost twice the current level) without any further capital increase. Loans outstanding amount to $105 billion and this leaves the Bank with a commitment authority of $79 billion. Net income in 1993 was $1.05 billion and total reserves and provisions amounted to $18.0 billion. Loan-loss provisions are 3 per cent of the outstanding portfolio, and the 8 countries in non-accrual status account for a total $2.5 billion or 2.3 per cent of the portfolio.

9   One-sixth was returned to members (Restitution Account) and one-sixth was sold in public auction to finance the Trust Fund.

10 Adams (1994), Mistry (1994), and Genberg (1994) have made comparisons between the build-up of the crisis of Savings and Loans institutions in the United States and the provision of concessional assistance by donors to enable countries to service their debts to the IFIs.

References

ADAMS, Patricia (1994), "The World Bank's Finances: An International S&L Crisis", *Policy Analysis*, No.215 (Washington D.C.: The Cato Institute).

GENBERG, Hans (1994), *Multilateral Financial Institutions and the Debt of the Severely Indebted Low-Income Countries* (Geneva: International Centre for Monetary and Banking Studies), May.

GREEN, Reginald H. (1993), "ESAF Renewal: Project Decision or Structural Entry Point?", in UNCTAD (1993a), pp. 29-46.

HORN, N. (ed.)(1985), Adaptation and Renegotiation of Contracts in International Trade and Finance (Deventer, The Netherlands: Kluwer).

IMF (1992), *Policies for African Development* (Washington, D.C.).

IMF (1994), *Official Financing of Developing Countries*, World Economic and Financial Series (Washington, D.C.).

IMF /World Bank (1995), *The Multilateral Debt of the Heavily Indebted Poor Countries* (Washington, D.C.), 6 February.

KILLICK, Tony (1993), "Enhancing the Cost-Effectiveness of Africa's Negotiations with its Creditors", in UNCTAD (1993a), pp. 1-27.

KILLICK, Tony (1994), *Issues in the Debt Situation of Low-Income Countries* (London: Overseas Development Institute), May.

MARTIN, Matthew (1993), *The Multilateral Debt Problems of Developing Countries* (Geneva: UNCTAD).

MISTRY, Percy S.(1994), *Multilateral Debt: An Emerging Crisis*? (The Hague: FONDAD), February.

Non-Aligned Movement (1994), *The Continuing Debt Crisis of Developing Countries*, Report of the Non-Aligned Movement (Jakarta).

Overseas Development Institute (1994), *Africa's Multilateral Debt: A Modest Proposal* (London).

SASDA (1994), *Evaluation of Swedish Development Cooperation with Zambia*, Secretariat for Analysis of Swedish Development Assistance (Stockholm: Ministry of Foreign Affairs).

UNCTAD (1993a), *International Monetary and Financial Issues for the 1990s*, Vol. III (UNCTAD/GID/G24/3) (New York: United Nations).

UNCTAD (1993b), *Trade and Development Report*, 1993 (New York: United Nations Publication, Sales No. E.93.II.D.10).

WORLD BANK (1992), *Report of the Portfolio Management Task Force* (Washington, D.C.), October.

WORLD BANK (1994a), *Toward Resolving the Debt Problem of the Severely Indebted Low-Income Countries (SILICs)* (Washington, D.C.), May.

WORLD BANK (1994b), *Annual Report* (Washington, D.C.).

Annex tables

Table A1

SIZE AND STRUCTURE OF THE EXTERNAL DEBT OF SEVERELY INDEBTED COUNTRIES, 1992

(Present value of debt as a percentage of exports)[a]

	Total debt	Private creditors	Official creditors	
			Bilateral	Multilateral (including IMF)
SILICs				
Burundi	430	12	108	309
Central African Republic	287	15	149	124
Egypt	178	35	124	19
Equatorial Guinea	368	0	290	78
Ethiopia	403	21	297	85
Ghana	245	35	70	140
Guinea-Bissau	2638	51	1773	814
Guyana	466	14	296	156
Honduras	264	28	92	145
Kenya	215	82	57	76
Lao People's Democratic Republic	438	2	294	142
Liberia	328	67	97	163
Madagascar	671	25	518	127
Mali	275	6	178	90
Mauritania	339	53	198	88
Mozambique	1157	36	1002	116
Myanmar	546	2	468	77
Nicaragua	2720	868	1612	240
Niger	338	68	169	101
Nigeria	219	26	169	24
Rwanda	298	35	80	182
Sao Tome and Principe	1174	107	662	406
Sierra Leone	593	264	200	129
Somalia	2557	41	1675	841
Sudan	2727	484	1777	466
Tanzania	790	26	564	201
Uganda	888	80	370	437
Zaire	452	50	321	80
Zambia	444	69	201	173
Selected SIMICs				
Bolivia	343	57	124	162
Cameroon	232	46	137	49
Congo	303	65	203	35
Cote d'Ivoire	453	264	119	69

Source: World Bank, Debtor Reporting System.

a Debt as of the end of 1992; exports are the 1990-1992 average.

Table A2

DEBT-BURDEN INDICATORS OF SEVERELY INDEBTED COUNTRIES, 1992

	Nominal value of debt stock (*$million*)	Nominal value of debt stock/ exports (*Per cent*)	Present value of debt stock/exports (*Per cent*)
SILICs			
Burundi	1023	948	430
Central African Republic	901	515	287
Egypt	40427	304	178
Equatorial Guinea	246	492	368
Ethiopia	4354	594	403
Ghana	4275	398	245
Guinea-Bissau	634	4030	2638
Guyana	1879	631	466
Honduras	3573	354	265
Kenya	6367	280	216
Lao People's Democratic Republic	1922	1793	438
Liberia	1952	358	328
Madagascar	4385	890	671
Mali	2595	483	275
Mauritania	2303	443	339
Mozambique	4929	1365	1157
Myanmar	5326	761	546
Nicaragua	11126	3068	2720
Niger	1711	477	338
Nigeria	30998	230	219
Rwanda	873	629	298
Sao Tome and Principe	190	2029	1174
Sierra Leone	1265	758	593
Somalia	2446	3216	2557
Sudan	16084	3006	2727
Tanzania	6715	1230	790
Uganda	2992	1452	888
Zaire	10912	556	452
Zambia	7041	567	444
Selected SIMICs			
Bolivia	4243	466	343
Cameroon	6554	273	232
Congo	4751	348	303
Cote d'Ivoire	17997	511	453

Source: World Bank, Debtor Reporting System.

GLOBAL FINANCIAL SYSTEM REFORM
AND THE C-20 PROCESS

Azizali F. Mohammed

Abstract

The paper identifies outstanding issues in international monetary and financial arrangements and makes the case for their review along the lines of the Committee of Twenty that worked during 1972-1974. The paper argues that the review cannot be restricted to a small grouping of industrial nations, given the wide-ranging ramifications of pending issues, and requires the full participation of developing and transition countries in approaches to their resolution.

The issues are classified as follows: (1) the exchange-rate regime; (2) the management of the global capital market; (3) the role of international reserve assets, including the role of the SDR; and (4) development finance and related issues.

In analyzing whether the composition and structure of the Committee of Twenty provides a model in current circumstances, the paper proposes that in the present environment of a market-dominated global economy, it would be essential that the debate extend beyond the official circles to include market practitioners as well as academics and think-tanks and other non-governmental organizations with serious interest in monetary and financial issues. With a Committee already enlarged to twenty-four to reflect the increased number of constituencies in the Bretton Woods institutions, the paper suggests the need for innovations in structuring the bodies responsible for analyzing the issues. It proposes the establishment of four working groups composed of official and non-official specialists to study and make recommendations dealing with (1) international monetary issues; (2) the management of private capital flows; (3) the decision-making processes in the international financial institutions, and (4) development finance and related issues. Their recommendations would be worked up by a central secretariat into proposals for decision-making at the political level.

I. Introduction

This paper argues that the present phase of discussions relating to reform of the international monetary and financial system has certain parallels with an earlier effort undertaken between 1972 and 1974. It raises the question whether the institutional mechanism deployed on that occasion for the preparation of reforms - namely the Committee of Twenty - offers a suitable model for launching an analogous exercise today. The paper supports the case for a "fully representative inter-governmental

participation" in the review process "in order to carry legitimacy, ensure a broad sense of ownership and be effective" (Group of Twenty-four, 1994).[1]

The "Ad Hoc Committee of the Board of Governors on Reform of the International Monetary System and Related Issues", known as the Committee of Twenty (C-20) was created by a Resolution of the IMF Board of Governors and worked from September 1972 through October 1974. Its composition reflected the constituency line-up of the IMF Executive Board of that time and represented a break from an earlier pattern of work on reform issues, which had been conducted in restricted groupings of industrial countries, notably the Group of Ten (see Annex 2). The preamble of the Resolution setting up the Committee stated that "decisions relating to the reform should be taken with the full participation of both developed and developing member countries". [2]

II. Parallels between current and C-20 reform efforts

In this section, four issues are examined with a view to determining whether they have been resolved, and if not, whether these, or analogous, issues call for another concerted effort towards their resolution. The issues selected for discussion are (1) the exchange-rate regime; (2) the management of global capital markets; (3) the place of reserve assets in the international financial system, and in particular, the role of the SDR; (4) development finance and related matters. In reality, these issues are inevitably interconnected; they are treated separately here for expository purposes.

A. *The exchange-rate regime*

At the time of the Committee's formation, there was a great deal of uncertainty, following the United States decision in August 1971 to suspend the convertibility of the dollar and emerging indications that the grid of exchange rates negotiated in the Smithsonian Agreement of December 1971 might not prove as durable as its protagonists claimed. Within the United States official establishment, a division of opinion was growing between Chairman Burns of the Federal Reserve Board, who believed, as did many central bankers in other industrial countries, that a reformed system could be based on a par value regime operated with somewhat greater flexibility, and Treasury Secretary Shultz, who along with much of the American academic community, favoured considerable flexibility for exchange rates and especially for the United States dollar.

It can be argued that, in the event, this controversy was settled in favour of floating exchange rates, particularly as between the United States dollar and the currencies of the other two principal industrial economies, Japan and Germany. Among other industrial countries, Canada was the first to experiment with a floating rate as far back as 1950; it was to be joined much later by Australia, New Zealand

and Switzerland; Italy and the United Kingdom opted to float in the aftermath of the crises of the European Exchange Rate Mechanism (ERM) in 1992-1993. Between 1983 and 1992, the share in trade of countries with floating exchange rates rose from 29 per cent to 45 per cent of the world total.

The IMF staff, who in the earlier exercise had displayed a strong predilection for pegged exchange rates, now argue that fundamental monetary reform - which they define as "a systematic and sustained effort on the part of the three major industrial countries to maintain their exchange rates within agreed ranges" - is "neither feasible nor desirable" (Mussa et al., 1994).

A major force propelling this view is the emergence of an increasingly integrated global capital market. It is argued that the growth of enormous pools of highly liquid private capital, capable of moving rapidly across national exchange markets, generates pressures that Governments are wholly unable to contain at acceptable political cost. In the future, therefore, "contingent policy rules designed to hit explicit exchange-rate targets will no longer be viable". [3]

Yet the issue can hardly be considered settled in an irrevocable way. The choice of exchange-rate regimes by the three major industrial countries is surely not a matter of indifference either to themselves or to a majority of other countries, whether industrial, developing, or the transition economies, who are constrained by that choice from having the option of participating in a global system of pegged rates. Among others, the present non-system carries costs in the form of excessive volatility of floating rates and periodic episodes of exchange-rate misalignment. The former injects vast uncertainty into the decision-making of economic agents participating in international trade and investment, thereby tending to reduce the potential volume of both. [4] Misalignments, as illustrated by the prolonged appreciation of the United States dollar in the mid-1980s and the appreciation of the Japanese Yen since 1993, result in major adjustment problems for the rest of the world economy through their large spillover effects. While the earlier dollar misalignment greatly strengthened protectionist forces in the world's largest economy, the current yen misalignment threatens to abort an uncertain recovery in the second-largest one. These are costs that need to be weighed carefully against the benefits of monetary independence that floating exchange regimes allow for the major countries, and the balance between costs and benefits could well be changing.

The character of the exchange regime remains an even more critical issue for policy-makers in a number of developing and transition economy countries that wish to use the nominal exchange rate as an anchor for dampening inflation expectations versus others that would use the exchange rate as an instrument of balance-of-payments adjustment.

Nor is there any consensus within the non-official establishment, as illustrated by the continuing support in influential quarters for different variants of the target-zone proposal; there is, in fact, a widespread expression of desire for a more stable regime of exchange rates.[5] Notable in this respect is the continuing advocacy on the part of more conservative elements for a return to something akin to a gold standard and an analogous argument for currency-board arrangements (for instance Shelton, 1994).

Even within the official community, there remain persistent questions about the wisdom of giving free rein to exchange markets that appear to go through identifiable phases of relative calm and relative turbulence and with a built-in propensity to overshoot. The "herding" instincts of private operators have caused bubbles, bank runs and panics in financial markets over the centuries, creating an ineluctable requirement for official intervention when crises occur. The modalities of greater international coordination of macroeconomic policies, as a means of achieving greater exchange-rate stability, remain a preoccupation of policy-makers in important countries, notably Japan and France.[6] In a real sense, the parallelism with the earlier debate on the exchange-rate regime persists, even if its focus has shifted somewhat from current-account considerations to the implications of capital mobility for the reform of the exchange-rate system.

B. Management of the global capital market

The problems created by the globalization of capital markets do not arise only in the exchange-rate context. Already at the time of the C-20 discussions, the subject of disequilibrating capital movements was a major issue. A Technical Group examined the sources of short-term private capital flows, the attempts made by various countries to control them and the possibility of coordinated action by groups of countries to manage them.

The debate has clearly moved further and it could be argued that in regard to a major component of the

earlier discussions, namely the efficacy of capital controls, the issue is moot. Industrial countries have almost completely eliminated controls on capital, as have many of the larger developing countries. The revolutions in telecommunications and computer technologies and the rapid evolution of financial systems have made it possible to move vast sums of money across borders at minimal transaction costs. This is especially true of portfolio capital, where the increasing securitization of financial claims makes it possible for large-scale investments to be made - and withdrawn - by an ever-changing cast of private owners of cross-border paper who buy and sell their claims in virtual anonymity.[7]

This change in the composition of capital flows makes financial crises harder to predict or forestall, and makes the management of private capital flows one of the major unsettled issues of the international financial system. The disorderly manner in which the crises of September 1992 and August 1993 in Europe forced the authorities of several member countries to abandon their adherence to the central parity grid of the ERM illustrates the power of large-scale private flows to throw off-track even countries with solid balance-of-payments positions, high reserve levels and extensive swap lines [8], sound banking systems and well-established regulatory arrangements.

Sudden changes in market sentiment caused by exogenous developments or varying perceptions about the soundness and consistency of macroeconomic policies result in a degree of volatility of capital flows for all countries integrating into the global capital market; this vulnerability is intensified for many emerging-market countries. The credibility of their macroeconomic policy frameworks tends to be weak, being of recent origin. Banking systems are fragile, having emerged from long periods of high inflation and State-directed credit allocation while supervisory institutions might only just be breaking free of egregious political interventions. Facilities for hedging risk are still evolving and access to derivative instruments is usually indirect. In conditions of large-scale "dollarization" resulting from the ability of both residents and non-residents to hold deposits or purchase financial claims denominated in foreign currency, the ability of central banks to act as "lender of last resort" is greatly reduced.

These weaknesses are reinforced by the vulnerability of emerging markets to changes in macroeconomic policies in the major industrial countries.[9] Such a change occurred in February 1994 when the United States Federal Reserve began to raise short-term interest rates, which resulted first in a slowdown in the flow of portfolio capital to developing countries and subsequently contributed to an outflow towards the end of the year. In light of the intensity of the ongoing Mexican crisis (as this is written) and its spreading "contagion" effects on other countries, particularly in Latin America, the problems created by rapid financial liberalization-cum-privatization need to be re-investigated for "the possibility of explosive paths or stagnant equilibria" (Fanelli and Frenkel, 1993). The entire issue of how to manage the enormous pool of volatile private capital flows so as to minimize their disturbing consequences for countries calls for a "no-options-barred" review that does not proceed from unquestioning judgements about the merits of unrestricted capital movements or the possibility of applying capital controls or the practicability of "sands-in-the-wheel" approaches to dealing with problems created by the global capital market as presently operating. [10]

The issues that need study are clearly broader and far more complex than at the time the C-20 looked at disequilibrating capital flows and suggest the necessity of a wide-ranging review by all the various interests, in developed, developing and transition countries alike, affected by the workings of global capital markets.

C. International reserve assets

1. National currencies as reserves

The C-20 agenda covered a number of issues relating to reserve assets, asset settlement, convertibility and consolidation of reserve currencies. Among the most contentious was the role of essentially two national currencies - at that time the United States dollar and the British pound - and their use as reserves and the need to find some way of dealing with the dollar and sterling "overhang" through consolidation (later referred to as "substitution"). Also on the agenda was the place of gold and the role of the (then) newly introduced international asset, the SDR.

The passage of two decades has resolved some of these issues and rendered others moot. The Second Amendment of the Fund's Articles dethroned gold as an official reserve asset and delinked the valuation of the SDR from it. While gold continues to be held as part of the reserves of many of the world's monetary authorities, there have been instances of central bank sales of a part of their gold stock (e.g. by the

Netherlands) at prices which are now determined, as for any other commodity, by market demand and supply. The issue of asset settlement for the United States has been largely emptied of policy content by the fact that the currency remains fully convertible at market-determined exchange rates, and those preferring to hold dollar balances presumably do so voluntarily, at market-determined interest rates. Although the pound sterling lost its reserve currency role in the late 1970s, the dollar has not become the sole reserve currency; both the DM and the Yen have acquired that status. The share of the dollar in official foreign exchange reserves has declined from about 80 per cent in the 1960s to under 60 per cent by the end of 1993, the result in part of currency diversification into the two other reserve currencies and in part to the declining value of the dollar relative to them. Whether this decline could reach a point where it triggers a sudden "flight" from the dollar remains one of the more unsettling questions in the prevailing non-system. Even absent such a "meltdown" scenario, the weakness of the dollar and excessive strength of the Yen have produced conjunctural tensions in the global economy by hardening interest rates on dollar-denominated assets (or preventing long-term dollar rates from softening as the United States economy slows) while impeding the recovery of the Japanese economy.

2. The role of the SDR

One of the few points of agreement in the C-20 was that the SDR should become the principal reserve asset of the reformed system, a sentiment enshrined in the Second Amendment; that consensus has since evaporated. There has been no new allocation since 1981; the SDR share in international reserves declined from a peak of 4.51 per cent in 1975 to under 1.90 per cent at the end of 1993 (see Buira, 1995). The future of the SDR became a source of contention at the Madrid Meetings of the Bretton Woods institutions in October 1994, when the Interim Committee failed to agree to an allocation proposed by the Managing Director of the IMF under the existing Article XVIII or to one proposed by the United States and United Kingdom delegations under an amendment of the Articles that would permit an SDR allocation not only to meet a global need for liquidity but also to correct an inequity in the SDR system by providing an extra margin of SDR to the countries that have joined the IMF since the last allocation was made. [11]

Whether there remains any prospect of finessing the objections of some of the principal shareholders of the Fund to any SDR allocation on the basis of "global need", the equity issue remains valid, and for a more important reason than that of fairness to the "new" members. The world is divided today between countries that have voluntary access to international capital markets and others that do not, the latter comprising the vast majority of developing and transition countries. This divide is apt to widen in the aftermath of the Mexican crisis as flows of private capital, especially of the portfolio variety, are reduced by its contagion effects. Many of the countries that do not participate in international securities markets have inadequate reserves - relative to imports - and can only add to them by reducing their net imports, which requires a compression of domestic demand "that would be inimical to their adjustment, reform and growth efforts".[12] An SDR allocation would enable these countries to reduce the risk of setbacks to these efforts by strengthening their reserves without having to curtail their import capacities.

The issue of the future role of the SDR, however, goes beyond considerations of inter-member equity or the most appropriate way of helping low-reserve countries. There is the possibility of a broader role for the SDR as a "last-resort financial safety net" [13] to help the IMF supplement its resources to meet exceptional demands, such as have arisen in the latest Mexican case (where a commitment of 688 per cent of Mexico's quota in the Fund was required). This type of financing need could be met through an incremental approach of creating SDR on an ad hoc basis to provide the Fund with additional resources to enable it to give sufficient credit to deal with liquidity crisis situations together with a clear commitment to cancel the ad hoc SDR issues when the Fund is repaid. A more ambitious approach would harken back to the original Keynes "bancor" concept or its more modern variant, namely an IMF based fully on the SDR (Polak, 1979), whereby the Fund could be restructured to create additional resources so as to provide conditional credit by means of the SDR technique.

Proposals for such a transformation of the Fund into a world central bank must begin to be considered seriously in light of the challenges posed by the emergence of the global capital market, including the desiderata involved in strengthening the SDR instrument to make it usable for intervention purposes on exchange markets. Given the recent acrimony between industrial and developing countries on the SDR issue, detailed studies and discussion need to be conducted jointly at the highest levels in both groups of member countries.

D. Development finance and related issues

The C-20 discussions focused on a number of issues of particular interest to developing countries, including the provision of financial resources for development through mechanisms such as an "SDR/Aid Link", preferential access for their manufactured products in industrial country markets and exemption from rules applied to industrial countries for correcting their balance-of-payments disequilibria or on the composition of their reserves. Two Technical Groups worked on "SDR/Aid Link and related proposals" and on the relationship between international monetary arrangements and "Transfer of Real Resources" to developing countries. While the work of the former group came to nought, [14] the second Technical Group's consideration of new institutional arrangements for the study of questions involved in resource transfers resulted in the setting up of a Joint Fund-Bank Ministerial group in the shape of the Development Committee, alongside the IMF Interim Committee, as successor bodies to the C20. The debate has since moved on to issues connected with the sovereign debt crisis of the 1980s, the debts owed to multilateral institutions and the decision-making processes of the international institutions.

The attaching of structural reform conditions to provision of debt relief and to concessional funding by the official agencies generates political resistance and even "adjustment fatigue" in aid-recipient countries; there is much concern about the growing tendency of the multilateral financing institutions to extend their conditionality to cover such sensitive political matters as "good" governance, democratic pluralism, demilitarization, social safety nets and legal reform.

Much current discussion is concerned with considerations of institutional change, such as the relationship of the Bretton Woods institutions to each other, that of the World Bank Group to the private sector and to regional development banks and also the relationship of the multilateral financial agencies to the World Trade Organization. The negotiations leading up to the establishment of the World Trade Organization surfaced conflicts of jurisdiction and the need for coordination with the Bretton Woods institutions, as the trade surveillance function takes on broader policy scope. At its core lies the concern that any trade liberalization process remains hostage to unpredictable exchange-rate fluctuations, brought about, as in the current Mexican crisis, by massive movements of capital.

The 50-year anniversary of the Bretton Woods institutions in 1994 provided an opportunity for renewed introspection as well as external scrutiny. The feeling that the two organizations have tended to undertake overlapping responsibilities in developing countries has dissipated somewhat, with the vast burden of helping the transition countries forcing both to a clearer division of labour. Proposals for merging the two continue, however, to issue from influential quarters [15] but given the much broader mandate of the Fund for the surveillance of the global economy and its rapid-response capacity for dealing with crisis situations, merger proposals are unlikely to make headway. [16] However, in a time of strong pressures for "downsizing" that affect official institutions across-the-board in the principal countries, a great deal of education of public opinion will be called for to allow these institutions the opportunity to adapt themselves to an environment of scarce budgetary resources and to the competition from private capital markets, to which their most successful clients have since graduated.

The issue is particularly difficult for the international agencies which must confront an additional hurdle: the recognition increasingly accorded to the principle of "subsidiarity" in international affairs. The regional European institutions have gained preferment, relative to the Washington-based agencies, in part from this trend, and the same tendency is operating in the context of regional groupings in other parts of the world. The World Bank Group must look for creative ways of relating to its regional counterparts, a subject of current examination by a high-level Task Force.

Finally, there is the growing weight of developing countries in the world economy and their desire to bring that weight to bear in the governance of the international financial institutions (IFIs). [17] How to guide the transition of these institutions in a market-dominated global economy, but in which political power is still exercised at national levels, constitutes a challenge that requires the urgent attention of the world community in a broadly representative forum and not in restricted groupings of industrial countries.

III. Is the C-20 model applicable under current conditions?

The preceding analysis has tried to highlight some of the unresolved issues in respect of

international monetary and financial arrangements that serve as the framework for the working of the IFIs. It has not sought to find solutions, but rather to indicate the urgency of tackling them at the highest levels of the membership. A similar challenge in the early 1970s led to the formation of the C-20, operating at the political level of Ministers of Finance and Central Bank Governors, and at the official level of their Deputies (Annex 2 lays out the organization of the Committee). The reasons for this particular construction have been carefully explained by the IMF Historian (de Vries, 1985, Volume 1, chapter 8). Here, it is sufficient to say that a Committee composed of IMF Governors could make use of the ready-made geographical representation embodied in the IMF/World Bank Executive Boards; it would not need weighted voting, being an advisory group; it could function with its own small technical staff, a high-powered six-member bureau; it could not be dominated by officials of the IMF/World Bank Group or other agencies that did prior work on the same issues, in the OECD, UNCTAD or the BIS; however, these organizations could be included in the deliberations.

A similar Committee today would have to be larger, if the same design were adopted, since the Executive Boards of the IFIs have grown to twenty-four to accommodate a range of new members from central Europe and the former Soviet Union, Switzerland, and a number of smaller States. This would, however, accentuate a defect of the C-20 structure that was characterized by the IMF Historian as "large and clumsy".[18] But in a world where private markets have taken on such an overarching role, it might be impossible to give credibility to an exercise undertaken solely by officials, so that the high-level groups would have to be even larger, if the same model were followed. Moreover, academic interest in international monetary and financial issues was always intense and has gained greater resonance with the entry of a number of think-tanks and public interest groups (covered under the rubric of "non-governmental organizations") and their exclusion would also detract from effectiveness.

It would thus appear that while the C-20 model might be a starting point for the process of review, it would not provide sufficient authority to its conclusions. Some more innovative formations, such as mixed groups of officials, market practitioners, academics and representatives of non-governmental organizations, could be constituted to study and report on specific issues, with a central secretariat attempting, in the manner of the C-20 Bureau, to formulate a draft that would be presented for decision by an apex political body.

At least four working groups, along the lines of the C-20 Technical Groups, but including non-officials, could be constituted to cover, respectively (1) international monetary issues, including the role of the SDR; (2) management of capital flows; (3) decision-making processes in the IFIs, and (4) development finance and related issues. The central secretariat would also have a mix of officials and non-officials but the apex of the structure would have to be at Ministerial level in order to develop the necessary political consensus, with their official Deputies preparing the legislative groundwork for amendment to the Articles of Agreement of the IFIs. Since amendments require high majorities to be adopted, the association of both developing and transition countries in the process leading up to them, must be provided for at all stages. It would not do for the G-7 countries to agree on certain positions and expect these to be accepted by the rest of the world community, as demonstrated by events at the Madrid Annual Meetings.

Notes

1 Annex 1 reproduces the relevant paragraphs of the communiqué.
2 De Vries (1985). The historical material in this paper draws on Chapters 8 through 14 of Volume 1.
3 The argument is not based solely on the emergence of capital mobility. The thesis is developed in the context of a "model in which the viability of international monetary arrangements hinges on three conditions: The ability to effect relative price adjustments, compatibility with the pursuit of robust monetary policies and a capacity to contain market pressures. In the future, changes in technology, market structure and politics will rule out the viability of any intermediary arrangements between floating and monetary unification" (Eichengreen, 1995).
4 The argument that exchange-rate risks can be hedged fails to recognize that such facilities do not extend beyond certain maturities, and that for many currencies, the markets have not developed sufficient depth to allow hedging at acceptable costs. The recent difficulties in markets for derivatives underline the indeterminate character of such costs.
5 See, for example, Volcker et al. (1994). The Commission recommends that G-7 Governments should strengthen the coordination of their macroeconomic policies with a view to achieving greater convergence and move to a set of credible commitments that "might include the establishment of exchange-rate bands".
6 Commenting on the Eichengreen thesis, Toyoo Gyohten, currently Chairman of the Bank of Tokyo and a former Vice Minister of Finance of Japan, argues that he had hoped for "suggestions on how to improve the relationship among major international currencies - a goal that he

dismisses too quickly as impossible" (Eichengreen, 1995, page 142). Similarly, the former French Prime Minister Edouard Balladur in an interview with Reuters on 14 March 1995 called for a return to a more managed currency system "similar to the Bretton Woods pegged currency system", adding that "the world economy courts disaster if major countries fail to stabilize their currencies".
7 Contrast this with the situation prevailing at the time of the sovereign debt crisis at the beginning of the 1980s when the major creditors were large international banks that had made term loans and were interested in maintaining a longer-term relationship with their customers.
8 Note that under ERM rules, currencies under attack had unlimited access to support from partner countries once these reached their outside intervention limits; the failure to maintain parities despite this open-ended commitment showed that market participants were well aware that sterilized intervention operates within the constraints of domestic bond and other financial markets and that unsterilized intervention creates monetary disturbances and generates financial market instabilities that cannot be sustained by partner country authorities for any length of time.
9 For an analysis of such vulnerability, see Mohammed (1994).
10 In this context, the revival of discussion of proposals for a "Tobin-type" tax is suggestive; the former French Prime Minister Balladur has proposed a system of deposit payments that dealers would have to lodge when making currency trades.
11 The developing countries through their eleven IMF Executive Directors, while supporting the Managing Director's original proposal, had submitted a compromise alternative for bifurcating the SDR allocation between an across-the-board allocation under the existing Articles and one that would achieve equity following an amendment to the Articles; that compromise was rejected as well.
12 In an address to the Institute for International Economics on 7 January 1994, the IMF Managing Director, M. Camdessus, pointed out that one in three developing countries and one in two transition countries have reserve levels below eight weeks of imports, with many holding reserves far below that level.
13 This concept appears in a recent speech of the Managing Director of the IMF delivered at the United Nations World Summit for Social Development, Copenhagen, 7 March, 1995.
14 While the Link proposals were taken off the agenda by 1985, the search for automatic mechanisms for financing developmental or environmental objectives has continued; among recent proposals is the use of "Tobin-tax" proceeds for social development, the international exploitation of deep sea mineral resources, renting the "Global Commons" etc..
15 The latest being George Schultz, former United States Treasury Secretary, at the 1995 annual meeting of the American Economic Association.
16 Some more practical arguments have been advanced by Stanley Fischer, then Professor of Economics, MIT. He rejects merger on the grounds that the Bank already "stretches the capacity of Management's control. The merged institution would be larger and more difficult to control. It would also be extremely costly to make the change. However, the most important reason to reject a

merger is that it would make the successor institution too powerful. Both the Bank and the Fund are now extraordinarily powerful in the smaller member countries" (Fischer, 1993).

17   Illustrative of the problem is the declining ratio of "basic" votes to total votes in the IMF. Each member country has 250 basic votes plus one additional vote per SDR 100,000 of quota. Successive quota increases have reduced the ratio from 12.4 per cent to less than 3 per cent, despite the entry of 138 new members compared with the original 44 members. Currently the Group of Ten countries plus Switzerland control 51.2 per cent of IMF voting power (Buira, 1995, fn. 17). In their Madrid communiqué, the Ministers of the Group of 24 "emphasized the need to find new ways for increasing the representation of developing countries and their effective participation in the decision-making processes of the Bretton Woods institutions" (Group of Twenty-four, 1994, fn. 1).

18   However, the Committee structure functioned much better at the Deputies level, with the head of the C-20 Bureau serving also as the chairman of the Deputies. Moreover, as the IMF Historian notes, while as many as 200 persons might have been in attendance at Committee meetings and a somewhat smaller number at meetings of the Deputies, "more than half were observers who did not speak; and ... various means other than general sessions were used - executive sessions, division into small groups and working parties - to permit debate and negotiation" (de Vries, 1985, Vol. 1, chap. 6).

References

BUIRA, Ariel (1995), "Reflections on the International Monetary System", *Princeton Essays in International Finance*, No. 195 (Princeton: Princeton University Press), January.

DE VRIES, Margaret Garritsen (1985), *The International Monetary Fund 1972-1978: Cooperation on Trial* (Washington, D.C.: IMF).

EICHENGREEN, Barry (1995), *International Monetary Arrangements for the 21st Century* (Washington, D.C.: The Brookings Institution).

FANELLI, Jose M., and Roberto FRENKEL (1993), "On Gradualism, Shock Treatment and Sequencing", in UNCTAD, *International Monetary and Financial Issues for the 1990s*, Vol. II (UNCTAD/GID/G24/2)(New York: United Nations).

FISCHER, Stanley (1993), paper presented to a conference on "The Future of the International Monetary System and Its Institutions", Geneva, International Center for Monetary and Banking Studies.

GROUP OF TWENTY-FOUR (1994), Press Communiqué of the Ministers of the Intergovernmental Group of 24 on International Monetary Affairs, *IMF Survey*, Vol. 23, No. 19, 17 October.

MOHAMMED, Azizali (1994), "Implications for IMF Policies Arising from Effects on Developing Countries of Industrial Country Macroeconomic Policies", in UNCTAD, *International Monetary and Financial Issues for the 1990s*, Vol. IV (UNCTAD/GID/G24/4)(New York: United Nations), October.

MUSSA, Michael, Morris GOLDSTEIN, Peter B. CLARK, Donald J. MATHIESON, and Tamim BAYOUMI (1994), "Improving the International Monetary System: Constraints and Possibilities", *IMF Occasional Paper*, No. 16 (Washington, D.C.).

POLAK, J. J. (1979), "Thoughts on an International Monetary Fund Based Fully in the SDR", *IMF Pamphlet Series*, No. 28 (Washington, D.C.).

SHELTON, Judy (1994), *Money Meltdown: Restoring Order to the Global Currency System* (Free Press).

VOLCKER, Paul A., Richard A. DEBS, Wilfried GUTH, and Yusuke KASHIWAGI (1994), "Report of the Bretton Woods Commission," April.

Annex I

Excerpts from the Press Communiqué of the Group of Twenty-Four, October 1994

"Ministers drew attention to the fact that developing countries are underrepresented in the Bretton Woods institutions, although they have been making a significant contribution to the growth of the world economy. They emphasized the need to find new ways for increasing the representation of developing countries and their effective participation in the decision-making processes of the Bretton Woods institutions and, especially, to strengthen these institutions, so as to ensure their continued effectiveness in supporting the development and adjustment efforts of these countries according to their national targets and priorities."

"In this context, Ministers took note of the Group of Seven industrial countries' (G-7) intended review of the framework of international institutions that will be required in order to meet the challenges of the twenty-first century, as announced in Naples in July 1994. They underscored that there should be a fully representative intergovernmental participation in such a review, on the general model of the Committee of Twenty of the 1970s, to evaluate the functioning of the Bretton Woods institutions and their future role in the context of a rapidly changing world economy. Ministers emphasized that such an evaluation should adequately involve the developing countries in order to carry legitimacy, ensure a broad sense of ownership and be effective. Ministers considered that the following topics should be included in the proposed review:

- The role that the IMF and the World Bank should play in ensuring that the management of economic policies is consistent with proper operation of the global economy;

- The working of the exchange-rate system with a view to reducing exchange-rate volatility and misalignments;

- The possibilities for enhancing the effective participation of developing countries in the decision-making processes of the Bretton Woods institutions. In this context the functioning of the Executive Boards of the IMF and the Bank, as well as the role, functioning and future of the Development Committee and the Interim Committee, should be examined;

- The appropriate forms of interaction between the Bretton Woods institutions and the regional financial and monetary institutions;

- The appropriate forms of interaction and division of labour between each of the Bretton Woods institutions and the World Trade organization (WTO)."

Annex II

Ad hoc Committee of the Board of Governors, IMF

Committee of Twenty
20 Members reflecting Executive Board Constituencies
(Ministers of Finance/Central Bank Governors)
Each Member has Two Associates
IMF Managing Director participates

Chairman:	Ali Wardhana, Indonesia
Secretary:	Secretary, IMF Executive Board
Advisors:	Executive Directors/Alternates
Observers:	BIS, European Community, Swiss National Bank, OECD, the World Bank, and UNCTAD

Committee of Twenty, Deputies
Each Member Appoints Two Deputies
(Senior National Officials)

Chairman:	C. Jeremy Morse, United Kingdom
Participants:	Executive Directors/Alternates/ Advisors; Senior IMF Staff
Observers:	BIS, European Community, Swiss National Bank, OECD, the World Bank, and UNCTAD

C - 20 Bureau

Chairman:	C. Jeremy Morse, United Kingdom
Vice Chairmen:	H. Frimpong Ansah, Ghana Alexander Kafka, Brazil Robert Solomon, United States Hideo Suzuki, Japan
Member:	Edward George

Technical Groups
(Chaired by Bureau Members)

(1) SDR/Aid Link and Related Proposals;
(2) Indicators;
(3) Disequilibrating Capital Flows;
(4) Adjustment;
(5) Global Liquidity and Consolidation;
(6) Intervention and Settlement;
(7) Transfer of Resources.

A CRITIQUE OF
THE WORLD DEVELOPMENT REPORT 1994:
INFRASTRUCTURE FOR DEVELOPMENT

Raisuddin Ahmed*

Abstract

The World Development Report 1994 *focuses on the inefficiencies of management and the maintenance of infrastructural stocks and services, and the ways whereby these deficiencies can be removed or their incidence reduced. The* Report *fulfils this task in an excellent manner, but the balance of emphasis and the overall tone of the* Report *reflect certain important deficiencies. This critique articulates these shortcomings. It is pointed out that, despite daunting measurement problems, infrastructural investments have played crucial roles in the progress of many developing countries. It is further argued that the* Report *suffers from urban bias, places lower emphasis on new investments than on the efficiency of existing infrastructure, falls short in its appreciation and articulation of the role of government and institutions in development, and does not fully explore the implications of infrastructural development in the alleviation of poverty. It is asserted that infrastructural investments must be strengthened in developing countries in order to supplement the ongoing forces of reform in the commodity and financial markets of the third world.*

I.   Introduction

The World Development Reports of the World Bank are an important source of information and guidance on topical themes of development problems. They are widely read and serve as informal guideposts for both the developing world and the donor community. The *World Development Report 1994: Infrastructure for Development* (in the following *WDR* or *Report*) holds immense implications for developing economies where infrastructural devel-

opment is perceived as being the basic fabric of political and economic integration and the foundation for economic growth and social development.

In order to avoid ambiguity and confusion, the *Report* defines infrastructure as including the following elements:

- Public utilities: power, telecommunications, piped water supply, sanitation and sewage, solid-waste collection and disposal, and piped gas;

- Public works: roads and major dams, and canal works for irrigation and drainage;

- Other transport sectors: urban and inter-urban railways, urban transport, ports and waterways, and airports.

The main messages and conclusions of the *Report* are as follows:

*   The author is solely responsible for the views expressed in this paper. Neither the Group of Twenty-four nor the Institute in which the author is employed, is responsible in any way for the views expressed in this paper. The author gratefully acknowledges the comments on an earlier draft from Professor Gerry Helleiner, University of Toronto, Canada.

- Infrastructure can deliver major benefits for economic growth, poverty alleviation and environmental sustainability - but only when it provides services that respond to effective demand and does so efficiently. Service is the goal and measure of development in infrastructure. Major investments have been made in infrastructure stocks, but in too many developing countries they are not generating the quality or quantity of services demanded. The costs of this waste, in terms of foregone economic growth and lost opportunities for poverty reduction and environmental improvement, are unacceptably high.

- Past investments in infrastructure have not yet had the developmental impact expected. The causes of poor past performance and the source of improved performance lie in the incentives facing providers. To ensure efficient, responsive delivery of infrastructure services, incentives need to be changed through the application of three instruments: commercial management, competition and stakeholder involvement. The roles of government and the private sector must likewise be reformed.

The theme of the *WDR* is efficiency. Infrastructure is often poorly built and managed in ways that result in waste and loss of production. One of the hallmarks of the *Report* is the effort to make the theme empirically valid, sufficiently convincing and adequately prescriptive to eradicate the identified ills. Another hallmark is the well-articulated argument for adopting various market mechanisms and involving private initiatives as antidotes to inefficiency and waste. The task set for the *Report* was heroic, and the staff carrying it out accomplished quite a lot in developing the main theme. The approaches to unbundling an entity of infrastructure into components that are marketable, and components that remain as public goods to be provided by government and the construction of a marketability index of various infrastructure are indeed very useful and analytically painstaking. This new direction in the treatment of infrastructure furthers the cause of market-oriented development, even though such efforts may be interpreted by some as being motivated by orthodox thinking. The *WDR* has endeavoured to develop a case of market reform in infrastructural services that can parallel the market reforms in commodity trade, financial and exchange systems under the structural adjustment programmes of the World Bank.

The *WDR* deserves credit for pointing out the many ills and inefficiencies in respect of the management and maintenance of infrastructural stocks and services and the ways by which these deficiencies can be removed or their incidence reduced. Nevertheless, the emphasis and overall tone of the *Report* reflect certain important deficiencies that reveal significant biases against the key role of infrastructure in economic development, particularly in developing countries. These shortcomings are articulated below. Despite the daunting problems inherent in the measurement of the impact of infrastructure, there is substantial evidence to support the crucial role played by infrastructural investments in the progress of many developing economies. It is further argued that the *Report* suffers from an urban bias, places less emphasis on new investments than on the efficiency of the existing infrastructure, falls short in its appreciation and articulation of the role of government and institutions in development, and does not fully explore the implications of infrastructural development for poverty alleviation.

II. Measuring the impact of infrastructure

Perhaps no other aspect of infrastructure is as important as the understanding of its actual impact. This is particularly so because many of the effects of infrastructure are indirect, something that is rarely acknowledged or appreciated. The *Report* rightly begins with this aspect (chapter 1), emphasizing the large potential impact. However, the *Report* concludes that "past investments in infrastructure have not had the developmental impact expected". Such a conclusion implies that the actual impact was not very impressive, but expectations remain undefined. The *Report* then presents evidence of an actual impact which, notwithstanding certain inconclusive features, appears to be quite impressive. Studies cited (box 1.1) show rates of return as high as 60 to 70 per cent. This is thought to be too good to be true. An analysis of World Bank projects demonstrates that the rates of return from infrastructural projects are higher than the average rate of return from other types of World Bank projects, even though the project evaluation approach generally fails to capture fully many indirect effects that are described below in the section on urban bias.

A recent survey of the literature provides an excellent summary of problems with the measurement of the impact of infrastructure (Gramlich, 1994). Drawing upon this and a few other papers extensively, we will briefly review the state of knowledge with respect to the measurement of infrastructural impact and its implication for the *Report*.

Broadly speaking, there is a macroeconomic and a microeconomic approach to measure the impact of infrastructure. The application of econometrics, particularly in the macroeconomic approach, plays an important role in such measurement. Under the macroeconomic approach, initial studies by Aschauer (1990, 1993) have been followed by many others, and a large amount of research has accumulated in this area. Macro-econometric studies involve a production- or cost-function analysis where the public stock of infrastructure enters as an explanatory variable. The initial studies found an extremely high rate of return (ranging from 60 to over 100 per cent). These results have been challenged on various grounds:

(i)   The variable "public stock of infrastructure" includes elements that have little to do with the particular productivity that is measured.

(ii)   The rate of return is too high. It is hard to see how the rate of return on public capital measured from output changes could ever lie above that of private capital. If public investment really were as profitable as claimed, would private investors not clamour to have the public sector impose taxes or float bonds to build roads, highways, etc., to generate these high benefits? Note that this question would be quite appropriate for developed countries where institutions are well developed to place pressure on exploiting the high benefit through bonds and other instruments. Developing countries, however, do not have effective institutions to exert such pressure and, therefore, higher rates of return from public capital stock are theoretically possible in developing countries.

(iii) The fact that some public capital has been productive in the past does not mean that future investments would also be productive. It is a reflection of the old problem of average versus marginal productivity.

(iv)   Does the change in infrastructure capital cause the change in output or does the change in output cause a change in the level of infrastructure? When both the stock of infrastructure and the production of goods and services in an economy increase in a parallel fashion, it becomes difficult to assign causality to either factor. However, as will be discussed in a later section, the direction of causality is not that complex in the context of developing economies.

Follow-up studies (see Munnel, 1992) have attempted to take care of the above objections and have found results ranging from a very high to an almost zero rate of return on public infrastructure stocks. The conclusion is that although most macro-econometric studies that are done carefully indicate a high rate of return on infrastructure, the results are often faulted on econometric grounds, and doubts persist.

The microeconomic approach to measuring the impact of infrastructure involves specific project evaluations (for example, the World Bank infrastructure projects reported in the *WDR*) and case studies of the type carried out by Ahmed and Hossain (1990) and reviewed by Ahmed and Donovan (1992). Microeconomic studies are quite rare and also suffer from limitations such as (i) a lack of representativeness of the aggregate system, (ii) an inadequate reflection of dynamic aspects, (iii) limitation in capturing spill-over effects, (iv) difficulties of separating effects of infrastructure from other factors. Nevertheless, most microeconomic studies demonstrate very high positive relations (the causality often flowing from infrastructure) between infrastructure, on the one hand, and output, employment, and income of the sample population, on the other.

What sense, if any, can be made out of the studies discussed so far? Macroeconomic studies are superior to microeconomic ones in that the former can capture many of the indirect and economy-wide spillover effects of infrastructure. Microeconomic studies on the project and village level cannot do that. However, econometric problems inherent in all studies, particularly the macroeconomic ones, are endemic and give rise to a number of questions. Some objections to macroeconomic results and the consequent corrective approaches seem to be seriously biased. One example of this is the objection to relating annual output growth to annual changes in infrastructural investment in order to correct for trend effects. Such models generate a zero or a very small rate of return on infrastructural investment. They essentially neglect the long-term impact and mainly measure the relation between short-run changes in infrastructural investment and output. But it is known that fully reaping the productive potential of investment in infrastructure requires much more time than is needed for other investments.

Perhaps the most valuable interpretation of the results of the different studies is that the microeconomic results reflect the minimum rate of return, whereas the macroeconomic results represent the upper bounds of rates of return, and that the real values lie somewhere in between. The rates of return as revealed in microeconomic studies range from 15 to 30 per cent; those revealed in macroeconomic studies range from 50 to 100 per cent. A range of 20 to 60 per cent seems to be the most plausible and any rate of return within this range may be termed as impressive. Given such evidence, it is difficult to conclude, as the *Report* does, that past investment in infrastructure has not made an impressive contribution because of inefficiency. Of course, contributions might be larger if the operational efficiency were greater, but a certain degree of inefficiency seems inherent in most developmental activities and investments.

III. Urban bias of the *Report*

The approach adopted in the *Report's* analysis of infrastructure does not differentiate between rural and urban infrastructure. Nevertheless, there is an implicit urban bias in the treatment of infrastructural issues in the *Report*. The list of infrastructure cited earlier includes irrigations and drainage canals. These are the only elements exclusively meant for rural-based production. Piped water supply, sanitation and sewage, solid-waste collection and disposal, piped gas - all are facilities that are primarily relevant to the urban areas of developing countries. It is, of course, true that roads and power supply could be sources of service for both rural and urban areas, but rural and urban roads and electricity supply have different dimensions and problems in terms of initial investment, maintenance, and management. Likewise, some urban infrastructure such as ports, airports, highways, etc., also make a contribution to rural economic activities, but this depends on the extent of rural feeder roads, rural transport and the communication facilities that connect rural and urban economies. This spatial aspect of infrastructural development has not been treated in the *Report*.

The existing system of infrastructure in most developing countries has largely favoured urban areas for certain fundamental historical reasons. Often, developing countries begin infrastructural development by connecting administrative seats of government with urban industrial centres. This priority may be motivated by the anxiety of Governments for national integration and industrialization. The pace of infrastructural development generally slows when the frontier of the rural hinterland is reached.

The *WDR* provides considerable statistics on infrastructure but without any breakdown between urban and rural sectors. On the impact of rural infrastructure the *Report* only gives citations from a few case studies (two from India and one from Bangladesh), all showing highly significant effects of rural infrastructure. Even though the strong impact found in the Bangladesh study is said to result form differences in the natural endowment of villages (which is incorrect in the sense that the methodology section of the cited case study explains precisely how land and soil-quality factors were confounded through appropriate designing), the potential of infrastructure to make a robust impact on economic development is recognized in the *Report*. The World Bank's project analyses are also cited to show a high rate of return, particularly on transport and communication infrastructure relative to other types of projects (*WDR*, p. 17). Nevertheless, the *Report* concludes that "for low-income countries, more basic infrastructure is important - such as water, irrigation, and (to a lesser extent) transport" (p.15). This de-emphasis of the role of transport is not consistent with the data on rates of return revealed in the *Report*. It probably arises from the urban bias of past development. Investment in this kind of infrastructure is crucial for rural areas. It can be observed that market centres, banks, public offices, schools, electricity supply lines, agricultural extension services and health centres in rural areas are usually located along transport and communication lines (Ahmed and Hossain, 1990; Saith, 1986; Binswanger et al., 1990).

A restatement of how rural infrastructure influences rural development positively, albeit in most instances indirectly, is thus warranted. Certain general hypotheses on the impact of rural infrastructure are presented below. They illustrate the balance of benefit-cost analysis that often appears to be the criterion for investment.

One of the most profound impacts of infrastructural development may be on the attitude and values of rural households, although such effects are the least visible to casual observers. Development of transport and communication infrastructure enhances the mobility of people and information through reductions in cost and time. The resulting increase in interaction with the outside world and the informal education process inherent in such interactions contribute to changes in attitude and human capital development. The effects of such changes are reflected, for example, in the increasing adoption of family planning practices (Hoque, 1987), diminishing faith in superstitions, increasing preference for consumer goods produced outside (Haggblade and Hazell, 1989), greater appreciation for formal education, and rising utility of income (Mellor, 1976). The effect on motivation - combined with the effect on entrepreneurial development that makes people more aware of and able to seize comparative advantages - bears immense implications for economic progress.

The positive impact of infrastructural development on reduction of marketing and transaction costs is well known. However, what is not fully perceived is the multi-faceted effect of infrastructural development on the expansion of markets, economies of scale, and improvement in market operations, particularly factor markets. The effect of infrastructure on market development is a critical link between infrastructure and commercialization, on the one hand, and commercialization and economic development, on the other.

The development of rural infrastructure helps to enlarge markets as it facilitates market access for actors on both the supply and the demand side. For one, easier access to markets allows an expansion of the production of perishable and transport-cost-intensive products, and, for another, it can lead to a conversion of latent demand into effective commercial demand. These effects of infrastructure are an important element of the commercialization process (Jaffee and Morton, 1995). Combined with the expansionary effect of specialization, they result in an increased scale of trade, and tend to reduce the trading costs per unit owing to economies of scale.

The effect of infrastructural development on labour markets is complex. Some features of related changes are the following:

- Availability of attractive consumer goods and income earning opportunities increases the tendency to work longer hours (Mellor, 1976);

- Participation of female labour in the workforce increases as traditional taboos against it are overcome (Rahman, 1994);

- The practice of bonded labour may diminish when alternative opportunities for labour are created by infrastructural development;

- Labour mobility improves and labour markets become less fragmented owing to infrastructural development; these changes result in increased

commercial transactions in labour markets and reduce the dualism between family and hired labour (Ahmed and Hossain, 1990; Haggblade and Liedholm, 1992; Hopkins and Berry, 1994).

The effect of infrastructure on agricultural production and diffusion of modern agricultural technology is mediated through a number of factors. First, because of the attitudinal changes discussed earlier, farmers in areas with developed infrastructure are more apt to accept new technology than those in areas with underdeveloped infrastructure. Secondly, marketing of modern inputs such as fertilizers, pesticides, and irrigation equipment is logistically easier and cheaper in infrastructurally developed areas. Agricultural extension workers find it convenient to work in places where they can move easily and live comfortably. Thirdly, both factor and product markets operate more efficiently in infrastructurally developed areas. The combined effect of all these elements results in increased agricultural production.

Increased demand for modern inputs, which are usually supplied from outside the agriculture sector, directly creates a demand for cash and exchange. This, in turn, indirectly creates pressure for the sale of farm products to finance the increased demand for inputs. The increase in production is generally associated with an increase in marketed as well as marketable surplus, thereby increasing the tempo of commercialization. In developing countries, where part of the agricultural production is meant for home consumption and part for sale, an increase in production leads to a more than proportionate increase in marketable surplus, partly because the additional production is usually not required for home consumption and partly because the demand for financing of purchased inputs and consumer goods increases (Chowdhury, 1994).

If infrastructural development is accompanied by policies permitting relatively free trade, then the effect on the production of non-farm goods and services in rural areas can be quite substantial. These effects are generally realized through an increased flow of consumer goods and services, increased processing of agricultural products in rural locations, increased flow of agricultural inputs and investment goods from outside the area, and dispersion of small-scale industries from urban to rural areas.

Among these factors, the effect of household expenditures on generation of demand for non-farm goods and services and the associated increase in employment is considered to be most profound.

Households allocate an increasing share of their total consumption expenditures to non-farm goods and services, owing to easier availability and lower prices of such goods and services in infrastructurally developed (compared to underdeveloped) areas, in addition to demonstration effects and the resulting change in taste. This shift is not limited to consumption items only. Investment patterns also change, owing to better housing, sanitation, water supply facilities and the acquisition of durable goods.

In view of the extensive implications of rural infrastructure for the rural economies of developing countries, it would have been quite appropriate (and consistent with the traditions of past World Development Reports), had there been special treatment of rural infrastructure.

IV. New investment versus efficiency of existing infrastructure

The message that management is the central problem, and that therefore both investment in improvement of existing infrastructure and the reform of its management constitute the principal challenge, tends to skirt around the issue. As already mentioned, the deficiency of rural infrastructure will require new and more investment than in the past. Because the agriculture/rural sector is still the largest sector in most developing countries, the growth of national economies will depend very much on new investment in rural infrastructure. In this respect, the *WDR* appears to have taken a backward-looking, instead of forward-looking, approach by not exploring the potential of future growth through new infrastructure investment.

The philosophy that such investment should be provided only when effective demand warrants such provisions is perhaps appropriate as a guiding concept for fully developed economies, and for certain types of urban infrastructure in high-income developing countries. However, it is largely invalid for low-income developing countries, and particularly with respect to rural infrastructure. Reliance on demand-led growth is, of course, very sensible in many commodity markets. However, the adoption of this principle in public investment for infrastructure may virtually reduce the scope for rural development and integration in most developing economies. Demand for infrastructure, particularly facilities linked to a wide variety of economic activities, can be effective only when collectively expressed. Such collective expression of demand is usually not possible in rural societies because of institutional deficiencies and weaknesses. Such deficiencies are quite rampant in certain parts of Africa and Asia; local institutions are believed to be better in Latin America for historical reasons. Moreover, ignorance of the complex relationship between infrastructure and the direct economic impact at the household level, and the paucity of information about opportunities beyond rural areas, make the formation of groups and the propagation of group interests very difficult in rural areas. In general, infrastructural investment has to occur long before the users can derive benefits or be in a position to discern effective demand. For these reasons, supply-side forces involving public initiatives do have a larger role to play in infrastructural development than implied in the *Report*. These may have been the considerations which moved Hirschman (1958) to suggest that a development-oriented government should create overcapacity in infrastructure, particularly where under- or unemployed resources exist. Infrastructural facilities might thus induce a higher level of economic activity.

However, one should not ignore that the management, improvement and retooling of inefficient infrastructure, or for that matter inefficient operation of public enterprises in general, represent serious problems in many societies. These inefficiencies must be addressed, just as new investment is needed for economic growth and development. Therefore, it is pertinent to examine the extent and nature of trade-offs between the reform of existing infrastructure and the creation of new facilities. Reforms of infrastructural policies and programmes as enunciated in the *WDR* have to go beyond a simple reduction of public involvement. Reforms will necessitate greater institutional support in terms of political commitment as well as regulatory institutions and devices for the privatization of facilities. The demand for human resources for implementing reforms will undoubtedly crowd out the need for public attention to remove constraints for new investment for rural and other productive infrastructure in developing countries.

V. Governance and institutional issues

Perhaps the key constraint for rural infrastructure development, and for rural areas in general, is the absence of effective operation of local government. These institutions barely exist in most developing countries, although the situation may be better in Latin America than in Asia and Africa. In

South Asia, "Union panchayets" and district councils exist in name, but are far from having the stature of effective government. These institutions do not share any resources under any constitutional arrangement and therefore do not have the capacity to develop and maintain rural infrastructure, which can hardly be done by a central government. Ruttan (1984) is one of the few authors who have emphasized the crucial role of local governments in determining the success or failure of rural development. The importance of local governments is, of course, reflected in exhortations for political, financial, and administrative decentralization (Wasylenko, 1987; Bahl and Nath, 1986; Levin, 1991). Ruttan points to the failure "to understand the difference between decentralized administration and decentralized governance - between locating administrative offices of central ministries at provincial or district levels and the strengthening of the fiscal and administrative capacity of local governments". This distinction is crucial. The important role of local governments in the maintenance of rural roads and markets has been documented from field experiences of major donors (USAID, 1987, for example). The key factor is the institution rather than the resource constraint. For example, Bangladesh currently collects about TK 250 million annually in land taxes against an assessed value of TK 600 million. The collection cost of this tax is, however, almost TK 250 million. If this collection of land taxes were transferred to local governments (assuming such bodies existed), the rate of collection would improve and the cost of collection would decrease. Such sources of revenue, supplemented by local property taxes and user fees on infrastructure services, could conceivably finance the operation of local governments to develop rural infrastructure and other facilities - the key requisite is a strengthening of local government.

It must be added that development of effective local governments will neither be quick nor easy. What, then, should be the strategy, at least in the interim period, before ideal local government institutions take root? Perhaps a second-best approach is in order, involving modification and strengthening of whatever institutions do exist and using them to implement a focused programme of infrastructural development.

Resources from central governments will continue to be the mainstay of financing for most infrastructural developments in contemporary developing countries. In reality, the allocation of resources at the central level depends very much on the strength of the constituent government

departments. In most developing countries there is no specialized department for rural infrastructure, while in some countries rural development departments may exist with a functional jurisdiction which usually does not include responsibility for rural transport and communication. For this reason, many donor-funded agricultural projects include components of rural infrastructure such as a part of development projects under an agriculture department, although the latter is generally an institution oriented to the development of agricultural commodities. Infrastructural development is often not suited to the outlook and skill of a traditional agriculture department. In order to ensure a smooth flow of resources from central governments to develop rural infrastructure, a specialized agency at the central level may be needed. This would be one of the elements of a second-best approach.

The *WDR* is, in our view, weak on the types of institutional issues discussed. Some general statements on the questions of decentralization and user participation are made in chapter 4 of the *Report* but these are couched in such general terms that the rural context and its associated needs are likely to be lost in the generality of the discussion.

VI. The roles of the public and the private sector

One of the central issues in infrastructural development concerns the question of the appropriate role of government in the provision and operation of infrastructure. On both theoretical and practical grounds, these tasks have historically been in the public domain. However, most construction tasks are generally carried out by private contractors on the basis of competitive bidding. The *WDR* makes a strong case for limiting the role of government to regulatory matters, privatization, introduction of commercial principles into management, attracting foreign firms for the development and management of infrastructure, etc.. Such reforms are shown to yield enormous savings in resources and an improvement of efficiency. The *Report* outlines four model options: (a) public ownership and public operation, (b) public ownership and private operation, (c) private ownership and private operation, and (d) community and user provision.

The concept of the private sector creating and operating infrastructure in developing countries is formulated and illustrated with selected examples presented in boxes. This form of presentation enables a short story to be told in an extremely concise fashion. Without proper analysis, however, the underlying reasons for success are rarely elucidated. Many questions warrant serious analysis before making generalizations, for example, whether the apparent success of a private-sector infrastructural entity is really a product of the private sector or if the hidden strong hand of public support is responsible for sustaining such an entity; and why success stories are not replicated in other places within the same country, not to mention other countries? It is widely known that the cooperative movement, once so widely advocated, has failed in the developing world, although it is not impossible to cite cases of success with cooperatives here and there.

While government failure is widespread and has been taken as a reason to reduce the role of the public sector, the need for a minimum role of the State as, for example, in regulatory matters for infrastructure, has never been denied. What happens, for example, when a corrupt public regulator colludes with a natural monopolist? Is the net social gain from a system with an inefficient public regulator and a private natural monopoly greater than the social gain from a system with only a public monopoly? The point is that the need for government in developing skills, capability and an efficient public administration cannot easily be substituted for. Contemporary attacks against the role of the government in development may have been carried too far, harming the cause for a harmonious balance between the private and the public sector. The *WDR* devotes little space to the examination of questions related to the improvement of public administration and institutional reform necessary for infrastructural development. Some readers may interpret these deficiencies as reflecting an ideological bias. The indication in the *Report* that rural infrastructure is primarily a matter for the local community to handle (option D) also serves to provoke such an interpretation.

The *WDR* attempts to chart a new direction in the development, operation and management of infrastructure. This new direction, as indicated earlier, is based on the involvement of private firms and the application of commercial principles, i.e. profit-oriented approaches in the construction and management of infrastructure. The old idea that the public sector has to play a predominant role in the provision of public goods is called into question. The charting of a new direction has, of course, driven the authors to "unbundle the broad functional element of infrastructure" into degrees of marketable and non-

marketable components. This immediately reminds the reader of the fundamental question of economies of scale. In the old approach to infrastructural development the important role of the public sector rested on the principle that the provision of most infrastructure was a natural monopoly so that a single agency was required to exploit economies of scale. Will the "unbundling of infrastructure" compromise the scope of exploitation of economies of scale in the new approach? If so, would the gain in efficiency resulting from an "unbundling and competitive marketing of infrastructure" exceed the loss due to inefficiency of the public enterprise? In the absence of answers to these questions, the new direction could be a hastily conceived idea that, even with its many positive aspects, might have limited appeal.

VII. Poverty and infrastructure

Lipton (1977) demonstrated that rural poverty was the source of deprivation among people in most developing countries. Measures that increase rural production, income and employment were, therefore, generally expected to contribute to the alleviation of poverty. Correction of the urban bias of past development policies, including the provision of infrastructure, will be a step towards poverty alleviation. Concern for poverty alleviation through infrastructural investment can be tested by the weight of rural components in the aggregate picture. As discussed above, these tests do not seem to indicate that the links between poverty and infrastructural development are considered very seriously in the *WDR*.

Perhaps it is not desirable to link every policy to poverty, simply following a popular fad. However, the link between rural infrastructure and the potential alleviation of poverty is already known to be too robust to be dismissed as a fad. The poverty profile of Bangladesh, for example, and an analysis of the impact of rural infrastructure on occupations in which most of the poor in that country are employed, provide some evidence on the links between poverty alleviation and infrastructural development (Ahmed and Hossain, 1990). Landless farm workers, small farmers, rural households working in the informal non-farm sector, and urban households working in the informal urban sector constitute the bulk of the poor in Bangladesh. Together, they represent half of the population of the country. Analysis of the contribution of infrastructure indicates that crop income among small farmers increases twice as fast in infrastructurally developed villages as in underdeveloped villages. Employment of hired labour increases threefold in areas with developed infrastructure as compared to underdeveloped villages, even though the overall increase in employment is small. However, increases in income from non-farm trade and business are much higher in rich households than in poor ones, mainly because of the capital constraints of poor households.

Other studies have demonstrated that infrastructural endowments were critical for the diversification of income among poor rural households in Niger and Senegal (Reardon and Kelly, 1993). Such diversification helped poor households to cope with crises resulting from natural disturbances. A recent study in Niger (Hopkins and Berry, 1994) has demonstrated that improved infrastructure can generate as high a level of income in low-potential areas as in high-potential areas, mainly because of the mitigation of the seasonal bottleneck in labour demand through the creation of a hired-labour market brought about by infrastructural development. The link between food security and rural infrastructures, based on empirical evidences from Asia and Africa, has been documented by Thimm et al. (1993).

The role of infrastructure in the delivery of relief supplies during a crisis is also well-documented (Ravallion, 1987; Alamgir, 1980; von Braun and Webb, 1994). The famines in Bangladesh and Ethiopia were partly the consequence of infrastructural disruption brought about by civil war. The afflictions as a result of famine were more intense in remote areas than in developed regions of the countries concerned. When famine afflicts a nation, and a government relief operation becomes a necessity, it is invariably the infrastructurally backward regions that remain outside its reach. The same is believed to be true in the implementation of regular public programmes for the rural poor.

VIII. Some miscellaneous points

An argument for more investment in infrastructure does not imply an inclination towards "the more the merrier" approach. Governments and donors constantly debate how much investment is appropriate and whether there is an optimal level of investment in infrastructure. Most evaluations of structural adjustment programmes point to infrastructural deficiencies as the root cause of a poor supply response in economies under reform. Almost all strategies for agricultural development in Africa

include infrastructural investment as a principal element (Delgado, 1994). The basic question of the adequacy of infrastructure remains as topical as the question of efficiency.

Developing countries generally use (a) an engineering approach, assessing needs on a technical basis; (b) a political process of consultation and popular demand; and (c) the rate of return from a project or category of projects as a way to assess the question of adequacy. These criteria cannot be claimed to be rigidly followed, but some combination thereof does provide a mechanism to resolve the question of adequacy. Are there better ways to guide public resource allocation for infrastructural development? The *WDR* seems to assume that this is an irrelevant question in the context of the general approach of demand-led investment that it espouses. However, as mentioned earlier, this approach ("feed the baby when it cries") often has many limitations in inducing an automatic investment response.

The economic rate of return has been historically used as a criterion for the selection of projects within a sector or across sectors, but such a criterion has not been very useful in overall resource allocation between directly productive investment and investment in infrastructure. The process of allocation is mostly driven by political forces and the perception of politicians of the importance of infrastructure. Economic analysis can exert a tremendous influence in this regard but this is not the point. The question is rather whether there is any objective basis to conclude that a given level of infrastructural investment is adequate or not? The issue is always present in most debates on infrastructural development in developing countries. Direct treatment of the issue would be quite useful in minimizing confusion in such debates.

The use of the measure of fiscal savings in judging the superiority or desirability of privatization of certain types of infrastructure seems to assume that privatization would not make any difference with respect to the aggregate developmental impact. This measure cannot be an adequate guide for the decision on privatization. In many developing countries, the so-called system loss in power supply is simply an indication that users are stealing electricity or of corrupt practices of public officials rather than real loss. Assuming that privatization will stop these practices, the aggregate demand for electricity and consequently the aggregate production of outputs based on electricity may also decline. This is not an argument against privatization but rather for the need of full analysis of costs, benefits and intergroup transfers before a case for privatization can be made.

One of the more serious concerns or lapses in guidance, other than those mentioned above, relates to the political and administrative feasibility of suggested reforms in infrastructure. The *Report*, of course, exhorts the need for political commitment. However, political reality warrants some strategies that politicians can depend on to build national commitment. Would some sort of sequencing of reforms help? What would be the pattern of such a sequencing? The institutional changes implied in the reform proposals are not clearly mentioned. The evolution of a public utility parastatal into a regulatory body cannot be brought about without some idea of the regulatory and other measures needed. These issues are either ignored or mentioned only casually in the *Report*, so that they will most likely escape notice.

IX. Concluding observations

In spite of persisting doubt, which will continue because of the very nature of infrastructure, the impact of infrastructure could be potentially very large and has actually been quite impressive in the past. The degree of realization of its full potential impact, however, depends on the policy environment within which infrastructural facilities operate to support mainstream economic and social activities. If a good network of roads is developed while at the same time restrictive policies do not allow private entrepreneurs to import appropriate vehicles to use the road, or government policies do not permit the movement of commodities between deficit and surplus areas, having such a good road network is not going to produce the desired results.

The 1980s witnessed a vigorous drive in developing countries for economic liberalization, aiming at creating a market-friendly environment. However, underdeveloped infrastructure in many countries, particularly in Africa, has not been conducive to generating the desired supply response that most people expected from these policies. In some cases, liberalization itself could not be carried out to the full extent because of perceived market failures, which can partly be attributed to underdeveloped infrastructure. Infrastructure and market liberalization policies are essentially complementary.

This complementarity implies that the past impact of infrastructural investment could have been

even larger had there been lesser degrees of control, regulation and intervention in markets that warranted structural adjustment in the first place. Now that structural adjustment programmes have started the process of market liberalization in developing countries, it is strategically crucial for infrastructural development to strengthen the functioning of markets in order to accelerate economic growth and the alleviation of poverty. The clarion call in the *WDR* for an improvement in the efficiency of existing infrastructural facilities should not blind us to the need to correct the imbalances in infrastructural stock between rural and urban sectors through increased new investment. Moreover, new investment in public infrastructure would most likely be critical for facilitating the transformation of developing economies from self-sufficiency-driven modes of production to export-oriented systems.

Improving the efficiency of infrastructure is, however, very important, and the developing countries should not dismiss the ideas for various improvements which are quite extensively developed in the *WDR*. But the privatization of some infrastructure and the introduction of a widespread competitive process in the development and management of infrastructure will take time. If this process is artificially forced to accelerate, there could be a real trade-off between reform and new investment. For developing countries, the new investment priority holds greater weight than the improvement of efficiency, although both are very important.

Structural adjustment programmes in developing countries have stipulated the need for ending the role of government in direct production and marketing activities, in addition to correcting for overvaluation of exchange rates and liberalization of trade regimes, so that Governments could give greater attention to infrastructural development. This line of thinking seems to have lost ground, as evidenced by decreased public expenditures in recent years, in spite of some success in the implementation of structural adjustment programmes. The *WDR* cites instances of such cases, such as the deterioration of roads in Africa, although the overall trend has been positive. It is, therefore, necessary to re-evaluate the public expenditure policies of developing countries. A reduced level of total public expenditure in order to support macroeconomic stability does not necessarily mean that allocation to infrastructure must drop *pari passu*. On the contrary, logically this allocation should increase.

For the infrastructural sector to be able to play an effective role in supporting the productive sectors of a liberalized economy, it is necessary for Governments to be forward-looking. Assessment of potential demand for infrastructure, followed by the creation of the respective facilities, will convert potential demand into effective demand. This is the sequence that the Governments of developing countries should be pursuing.

References

AHMED, Raisuddin, and M. HOSSAIN (1990), "Development Impact of Rural Infrastructure in Bangladesh", *Research Report*, No. 83 (Washington, D.C.: International Food Policy Research Institute).

AHMED, Raisuddin, and C. DONOVAN (1992), *Issues of Infrastructural Development: A Synthesis of the Literature* (Washington, D.C.: International Food Policy Research Institute).

ALAMGIR, M. M. (1980), *Political Economy of Mass Starvation* (Cambridge, MA).

ASCHAUER, David A. (1990), "Why is Infrastructure Important", in Alicia M. Munnel (ed.), *Conference Series*, No. 24 (Boston, MA: Federal Reserve Bank).

ASCHAUER, David A. (1993), "Genuine Economic Returns to Infrastructure Investment", *Journal of Policy Studies*, Vol. 21.

BAHL, R., and S. NATH (1986), "Public Expenditure Decentralization in Developing Countries", *Environment and Planning*, C-4.

BINSWANGER, Hans, S. KHANDAKAR, and M. ROSENZWEIG (1989), "How Infrastructure and Financial Institutions Affect Agricultural Output and Investment in India", *World Bank Working Paper*, No. 163 (Washington, D.C.).

CHOWDHURY, Nuimuddin (1993), "Determinants of Consumption and Marketed Surplus of Rice among Farm Households of Bangladesh", *Working Paper, Bangladesh Food Policy Project* (Washington, D.C.: International Food Policy Research Institute).

DELGADO, Christopher (1994), "Contrasting Perspectives on Agricultural Development Strategy in Africa Since the 1960s", paper presented to the IFPRI's 2020 Conference in Senegal, December (Washington, D.C.: International Food Policy Research Institute).

GRAMLICH, Edward M. (1994), "Infrastructure Investment: A Review Essay", *Journal of Economic Literature*, Vol. 32, No. 3.

HAGGBLADE, Steve, and Peter B.R. HAZELL (1989), "Agricultural Technology and Farm-Nonfarm Growth Linkages", *Agricultural Economics*, Vol. 3.

HAGGBLADE, Steve, and Carl LIEDHOLM (1992), "Agriculture, Rural Labour Market, and Evolution of Rural Nonfarm Economy", in *Sustainable Agricultural Development: The Role of International Cooperation*, Proceedings for the Twenty-first International Conference of Agricultural Economists, August 1991, Tokyo (Vermont: Dartmouth Publishing Co).

HIRSCHMAN, Albert O.(1958), *Strategy of Economic Development* (New Haven, CT: Yale University Press).

HOPKINS, Jane, and Philippe BERRY (1994), *Determinants of Land and Labour Productivity in the Agriculture of Niger*, Report to USAID (Washington, D.C.: International Food Policy Research Institute).

HOQUE, Nazyul (1987), *Rural Electrification and Its Impact on Fertility: Evidence from Bangladesh* (Pennsylvania State University).

JAFFEE, Steven, and John MORTON (eds.) (1995), *Marketing Africa's High-Valued Foods* (Dubuque, Iowa: Hunt Publishing Co).

LEVIN, J. (1991), "Measuring the Role of Sub-National Governments", *IMF Working Paper* (Washington, D.C.: IMF, Fiscal Affairs Department).

LIPTON, M. (1977), *Why Poor People Stay Poor: A Study of Urban Bias in World Development* (Cambridge, MA: Harvard University Press).

MELLOR, John W. (1976), *The New Economics of Growth: A Strategy for India and the Developing World* (Ithaca and London: Cornell University Press).

MUNNEL, Alicia H. (1992), "Infrastructure Investment and Economic Growth", *Journal of Economic Perspectives*, Vol. 6, No.4 (fall).

RAHMAN, Rushidan Islam (1993), "A Review of the Findings of Labour Force Surveys and Their Analytical Basis", *Bangladesh Development Studies*, Vol. 21, No. 1.

RAVALLION, Martin, (1987), *Markets and Famines* (London: Clarendon Press).

REARDON, Thomas, and Valerie KELLY (1993), *Agricultural Policy Reform Impacts in Senegal*, Report to USAID (Washington, D.C.: International Food Policy Research Institute).

RUTTAN, V. (1984), "Integrated Rural Development Programs: A Skeptical Perspective", *International Development Review*, Vol. 17, No. 4.

THIMM, Heinz-Ulrich, Herwig HAHN, and D. SCHULTZ (eds.) (1993), *Regional Food Security and Rural Infrastructure* (Hamburg: Lit Verlag).

USAID (1987), *Rural Infrastructure Project Identification Document*, AID Project No. 492-0420.

VON BRAUN, Joachim, and Patrick WEBB (1994), *Famine and Food Security in Ethiopia: Lessons for Africa* (London: Wiley Publishing).

WASYLENKO, M. (1987), "Fiscal Decentralization and Economic Development", *Public Budgeting and Finance* (winter).

WORLD BANK (1994), *World Development Report, 1994: Infrastructure for Development* (Oxford: Oxford University Press).

LABOUR ISSUES IN THE WORLD DEVELOPMENT REPORT: A CRITICAL ASSESSMENT

Dipak Mazumdar

Abstract

The article reviews the first three of the four parts of the World Development Report 1995 (WDR). No comments have been made on the last part because it was felt that the limited space given to the labour market problems in transition economies was simply not sufficient for an informative assessment of these problems. After all, the World Development Report 1996 will be entirely devoted to the problems of transitional economies.

In its first part, on Labour and Development Strategy, the WDR 1995 fails to articulate and discuss a model of the labour market specifically applicable to developing countries. It does not give adequate emphasis on development policies that might improve the living standard of workers in the third world. Some basic aspects of the labour market scene in developing countries, like segmentation, surplus labour and the informal sector have just been treated as additions to the story, instead of occupying the central stage. The implicit model of a homogeneous labour market leads to an overemphasis on the formal sector, which constitutes only a small part of the labour market in developing countries. As in textbook models of a homogeneous labour market with an inelastic supply of labour, the conditions for an improvement of wages are seen to be increasing the demand for labour in the formal sector. Hence the WDR's emphasis on export growth, particularly of manufactured goods. With a vast reservoir of surplus labour in agriculture and the informal sector in the developing world, the key to raising workers' earnings in these economies is to increase the supply price of such labour - and this can only be done with policies that augment labour productivity in agriculture. In many cases overemphasis on export growth might detract from this objective.

Other aspects of export growth and labour incomes dealt with in this review include the continued importance of exports of primary commodities for developing countries, and the impact of the fall in the terms of trade of such products in the 1980s. The evidence of globalization leading to growing inequality in the distribution of incomes between regions and within individual countries or regions is also discussed.

Finally, the impact of labour regulation on both the formal and the informal sectors in developing countries, is taken up.

Introduction

The *World Development Report 1995* (World Bank, 1995, hereafter referred to as the *Report* or *WDR*) covers a large range of topics in the area of employment. It impresses by width rather than the depth of its coverage. There are four parts:

(1) Development strategy and increase in workers' incomes;

(2) International integration and its implications for workers' standard of living;

(3) Labour standards and the regulation of labour markets; and

(4) Problems of adjustment and transition.

The first section of this review is devoted to a critical assessment of the implicit model of labour markets within which the *WDR* operates.

In section II, the impact of trade, particularly current patterns of "globalization", on workers' standard of living will be examined. The *WDR* gives pride of place to export-oriented development strategy as the most effective way to raise the standard of living for workers around the world. It expounds the virtues of this strategy as the current alternative to what it considers to be the outdated and disgraced strategy of inward-looking development with State-supported industrialization. In part 2 of the *WDR* the picture of an integrated world economy, with countries linked by trade and factor mobility, is presented as an established scenario of contemporary development. It is interesting to see that *World Employment 1995*, the first employment report of the International Labour Office (ILO, 1995), published almost simultaneously, opens its discussion with a long chapter on "globalization" and its implications for employment and labour earnings. However, the analysis of trade patterns and globalization in both reports - but perhaps more so in the *WDR* - suffers from overenthusiasm about the emerging trends in the international economy. As a consequence, some basic problems of their impact on employment and labour incomes in the developing world have been glossed over or not mentioned at all.

Finally, in section III we discuss critically the *WDR* assessment of issues of labour regulation. Paradoxically, of the two reports, it is the *WDR* that pays more attention to this set of problems. The ILO document treats the problems only briefly in the separate chapters on developing countries and the formerly socialist economies.

The *WDR* discusses labour market problems of adjustment and transition in its last part. We have deliberately refrained from treating these issues at any length. A proper evaluation requires an extended assessment of the experience with adjustment and transition policies pursued in different parts of the world. The *WDR* itself did not have sufficient space for such an exercise.[1] We make brief references to the more important labour market experiences under these policy regimes at appropriate places in the review.

I.   Labour and the development strategy

The *WDR* is really concerned with the issues of employment rather than the functioning of labour markets. The latter is touched upon at many points,

but since it is not placed at the centre of the stage, the *Report* is not distinguished by any serious consideration of the prevalent and peculiar characteristics of labour markets of developing countries. This omission, which indeed might have been a deliberate decision taken early on by the group overseeing the preparation of the *WDR*, has implications for some of the analysis and conclusions presented. In the absence of a specified model of labour markets for developing countries, the *Report* has had to fall back, time and again, upon a simple model to be found in standard text books. This is the model of a homogeneous labour market with an inelastic supply of labour, where demand conditions alone determine the price of labour (wage). It will be seen in the subsequent discussion that the possibly unconscious adoption of this paradigm has at several points led to imperfect and even misleading conclusions, and to an inadequate presentation of key factual information on the employment scene in developing countries.

A.   Non-homogeneous labour markets

The *WDR* begins with a succinct description of labour market outcomes in economies with different levels of income. The shift in the structure of employment from agriculture towards industry and services is well known and is re-established in Figure 1.1 on the basis of cross-section data from high-, middle- and low-income countries. The figure hides some important issues in the differences in the structure of employment. Of greater interest is Figure 1.2 (p. 11) which portrays the difference in workers' earnings in a few occupations in selected cities of the world. The figures in local currency are converted to dollars at purchasing power parity. This is all to the good and shows the enormous difference in earnings between cities even when the conversion rate allows for differences in cost of living.

But apart from making this general point, the discussion falters when it comes to suggest an explanation for the observed pay differences. "Differences in labor market outcomes", says the *WDR*, "can all be traced back to the productivity of labor - productivity referring to the quantity and value of labor's contribution ... Within occupations, pay differences across countries reflect the average level of *economy-wide productivity*" [italics in the original]. A question immediately arises about the meaning of "economy-wide" productivity. One could, of course, assume away the problem by thinking in terms of a single, homogeneous labour market - and this is what the authors of the *WDR* have presumably done. Otherwise, the level of economy-wide productivity has to be thought of as a weighted average of productivity in different sectors of the economy, in which case the differences in relative intersectoral productivity between countries is of central importance. In particular, the occupations referred to in Figure 1.2 are those found in the modern formal sector. Countries would differ in the extent of the gap between the level of earnings in this sector and those in agriculture and in the urban informal sector. The level of earnings per worker in agriculture would reflect the incidence of underemployment or "surplus labour" in this sector, given the state of development of agricultural technology in the economy. The earnings in the informal sector outside agriculture would be influenced both by the extent of underemployment in agriculture as it affects the supply price of labour spilling over into the former, and by industrial and other policies which define the role of the modern formal sector in the non-agricultural economy of the country concerned. The extent of the earnings

difference as between the three broad sectors is of major importance both for labour market outcomes and for policy.

The issues could be illustrated from the differences in the experience of countries of South-East Asia - a region which the *WDR* has identified as being characterized by policies which "mostly avoided sharp divides between modern-sector and rural workers" (*WDR*, p. 13, para. 4). Table 1 sets out the relative income per worker in the three broad sectors, agriculture, industry and services, in selected countries of South-East Asia in 1991. The distinction between industry and services do not in fact coincide with the division between the formal and the informal sectors. But since a great deal more of the workforce in the services sector is in the small-scale informal enterprises than the workforce in the industrial sector, the services-industry distinction is often used as a rough proxy for the informal-formal divide to indicate orders of magnitude in the absence of readily available data.

Table 1

SECTORAL INCOME AND EMPLOYMENT INDICATORS FOR SELECTED COUNTRIES, 1991

		Agriculture	Industry	Services
Republic of Korea	(1)	0.45	1.21	0.84
	(2)	*16.7*	*35.6*	*47.7*
Thailand	(1)	0.21	2.38	1.66
	(2)	*63.2*	*15.5*	*21.3*
Malaysia	(1)	0.61	1.46	0.73
	(2)	*26.0*	*27.5*	*46.5*
Indonesia	(1)	0.38	1.87	1.17
	(2)	*53.9*	*14.6*	*31.6*
Philippines	(1)	0.50	2.43	0.98
	(2)	*46.0*	*16.6*	*37.4*

Note: Row (1) gives the relative income per worker, row (2) the sectors' employment in per cent of total employment.

Source: The distribution of employment figures are calculated form the data published in the *ILO Yearbook* (1993), table 3. They are combined with the percentage distribution of GDP reported in the World Bank's *World Development Report 1992*, to obtain the relative income for each sector with respect to economy-wide GDP per worker.

Rough as these figures are, they do point to important differences between countries of the region in terms of labour market outcomes. Industry generally uses a good deal more capital per worker than agriculture, and the use of capital in services is probably in between the levels in the other two sectors. Thus, income per worker (which includes payment to capital) can be expected to increase from agriculture to services and from services to industry in most economies. But the differentials are substantially larger for some countries than others.

Taking the relatives for the Republic of Korea and Malaysia as being near to the average or the norm, Thailand and Indonesia had particularly depressed levels of income per worker in agriculture in 1991, showing the greater incidence of surplus labour in agriculture. Indonesia, or rather its most important island, Java, has long been considered to be characterized by the high density of population on land, with significant underemployment of labour in agriculture.

The situation in Thailand, although less known, is consistent with accounts given by Thai economists (Sussankarn, 1989). The problem in the agricultural economy of this country is accentuated by the prevalence of regional pockets of underemployed rural labour. In the Philippines, a major problem would seem to be the enormous gap in income per worker between the services (informal) and industry (formal) sectors. This is also consistent with the judgement that the incidence of "dualism" in the non-agricultural economy of the Philippines, as in many Latin American countries, is high because macroeconomic and industrial policies favoured a capital-intensive industrial sector with limited absorption of labour, so that a large part of the growing labour force had to find employment in the informal service economy, pushing incomes down in this sector.

In this small example, we already see points that should attract the concerns of policy makers. In spite of agricultural progress in recent years, in 1991 both Thailand and Indonesia required policies directed at absorbing underemployed labour in their farm sector. A special task for policy makers in the Philippines would seem to be industrial and other policies which would improve income conditions in the non-farm informal sector.

The *WDR* would have done a service by setting out, even with such simple statistics, the position of different regions and countries in sheltering underemployed labour in agriculture and services at low earnings relative to the modern sector. But the presentation of global statistics of employment-related issues is weak in this document. We will come back in more detail to this rather serious deficiency of the *WDR*, as indeed of other international reports on employment issues.

B. *The model of intersectoral earnings differentials*

A crucial issue for policy and other concerns is, of course, what causes the persistence of the types of earnings differential noted above. Implications for policy will vary depending on the diagnosis.

The *WDR* provides no extensive discussion of the issues and hypotheses which have been suggested in the literature. But given the importance of the topic, it has to take a stand on the question. The hypothesis it favours is suggested in chapter 4 of the *Report* under the section entitled "Labor regulation, labor dualism and the informal sector". The *Report* states: "Policies that favor the small groups of workers in high-productivity activities lead to dualism (segmentation of the labour force into privileged and underprivileged groups) and tend to close the formal sector off from broader influences from the labor market, at the cost of job growth" (p. 34). The *Report* provides no evidence for this view, but suggests that a labour regulation that protects formal sector workers occurs when output markets are "sheltered from competition by trade protection or public ownership".

Extensive research and experience exist to suggest that the view that the formal sector is created by labour legislation is a very restricted view of this widespread feature of developing economies. Large wage differentials between the formal sector in modern industry and the informal and rural sectors existed well before the era of labour laws and institutions in Bombay at the turn of the century (Mazumdar, 1973). Large formal-informal wage gaps are observed in countries with weak labour legislation or trade unions. It is clear that the extreme view propagated by the *WDR* is based on a simplistic theoretical model rather than on facts. In particular, this hypothesis ignores the impact of the introduction of high productivity modern technology on an economy characterized by traditional modes of production.

Although there is some substitutability between labour and capital in the spectrum of modern technologies, there is generally a minimum level of a capital-to-labour ratio which is operationally feasible.

Since this level of capital-labour ratio is often higher than that found in traditional agriculture or the craft economy, labour productivity is established at a higher level in the modern sector. The wage levels in the high-productivity sector are also established at higher levels relative to the traditional sectors, partly because of efficiency wage considerations as employers try to establish a committed industrial labour force, and partly through profit-sharing motives affecting worker morale and productivity. This is not to deny that institutional distortions in specific markets do accentuate the segmentation initially due to technology, but again it is wrong to single out labour market distortions as being the only or even primary factor.

This is borne out by research done in the evolution of East Asian economies, ironically a region which is excluded in the *WDR* from being in the purview of distorted differentials. Segmentation within the manufacturing sector, in the sense of a continued coexistence of large and small firms at different levels of productivity and wages, has been a feature of the Japanese economy since the beginning of its industrialization, and has in fact been accentuated over time. Detailed studies by Japanese and Western scholars have shown that the development of large oligopolistic firms with strong connections to the financial institutions accentuated the differentials in capital intensity and labour productivity between small and large firms. The high-productivity large sector found it efficient to superimpose a labour system on this industrial scenario which offered high wages to workers who were recruited at a young age and enjoyed lifetime job security in exchange for commitment to the firm.

Shinohara (1962) considered that each of the markets for labour, goods and capital, was indispensable to a full understanding of the dualistic aspect of the Japanese economy, but that the segmentation of the capital market played the most critical role. "We may safely speculate that capital concentration ... can be expected to be at the top in the following chain of causation: differential in capital intensity, productivity difference, wage differential".

The authors of the *WDR* probably felt that it was inadequate for a report on employment to consider distortions in capital markets. But this is ignoring the importance of interrelated factor markets in any diagnosis of economic phenomena. And if, indeed, capital-market distortion is the driving force in the accentuation of "dualism", the report could be seriously misleading in focusing as it does on labour market distortions. We will come back to this point in our policy conclusions in subsection E below.

C. *Economic growth and returns to labour*

The message of the *WDR* is that economic growth, meaning growth in GDP per capita, is the surest means of increasing wages. It suggests that this is almost a truism: "Gross domestic product (GDP) measures the value added by all factors of production - land, labor and capital - and wages measure value added by labor. If GDP per worker is growing, then value added per worker must be growing and under most circumstances so must wages". It will be recognized that the truism holds in a homogeneous labour market with an inelastic supply of labour. The level of wages is determined solely by the demand for labour. With capital accumulation the demand curve for labour is pushed upwards, leading to an increase in the average and the marginal product of labour. Unless there is a significant fall in the share of labour in total value added (which is theoretically possible if technological progress is persistently "non-neutral", but which has not happened in the long run in the history of modern economic growth), the wage per worker would increase *pari passu* with the average productivity of labour.

Alternative models of the labour market which have been discussed in the literature suggest more interesting questions and seek to elicit more useful data for tracing the evolution of labour markets and labour incomes in developing countries. The well-known Lewis model of development of the modern sector, for example, predicted that there will be a period of constant real wages in the modern sector until surplus labour was exhausted in agriculture, and only then would wages begin to increase, presumably at the same rate as average productivity of labour. Unlike the implicit model of the *WDR*, the Lewis model emphasized the importance of the supply curve of labour in wage determination in the modern sector. Other models of segmented labour markets discussed above would predict that labour earnings in the different segments of the market, in agriculture, the informal and the formal sectors, could move at different rates and even different directions, depending on the pattern of economic growth. It is important to obtain information on these possible trends in labour earnings, not only to judge the functioning of labour markets, but also to throw light on the changes in the economic welfare of different segments of the working poulation. One looks in vain in the *WDR* for any attempt to obtain information on such key issues of labour market evolution.

Figure 2.2 on p. 19 of the *Report* purports to demonstrate empirically the close association of GDP growth and wage growth. Although little detail is given in the relevant appendix about the nature and sources of the data, it seems clear that the statistics on manufacturing wages refer to organized (formal) enterprises reporting to the UNIDO database, while the agricultural wage rates cover a mix of plantation (again formal) sector and field-worker wages. The material does not cover the informal sector at all.

Furthermore, agricultural labour earnings are only partly a function of wage rates, the other significant variable being the number of days of work secured by a labourer over a period of time.[2] Statistically, the trend line shown in the scatter diagram is heavily influenced by the extreme values, as indeed are the individual observations plotted in the diagram. Evidently, the *WDR* team made a heroic effort at presenting some catchy statistical exercise rather than embark on a major effort to gather data on labour earnings in the developing world. The cop-out is serious, reflecting a deficiency in the work of international agencies concerned with collecting and reporting labour statistics in these countries. In the mind of this author, it merits emphasis in the special subsection that follows.

D. The wasteland of labour data in developing countries

In terms of the discussion of the labour market scene in developing countries, it is important to know the structure of employment and earnings of labour in at least three sectors: the farm economy, the informal sector and the formal manufacturing sector. As explained above, unless one makes the extreme assumption that labour markets are homogeneous, one cannot infer trends in employment and wages just from information on one sector. It is now possible to obtain information on the three sectors mentioned, and possibly some subsectors of them, from labour force surveys undertaken by national statistical offices in many countries.

Not all of these surveys are done on a predetermined regular basis, but it is possible to obtain information for a large number of countries by stringing together the results of labour force and household surveys over time. The *WDR* itself makes one such half-hearted attempt to look at earnings trends in the period 1973-1989 for some selected occupations for one country (Malaysia, table 2.2, p. 18). But the exercise was not comprehensive enough and is subject to criticism for ignoring the surveys of

intervening years in the period considered. In any event, the example of a few selected occupations in a single country cannot be generalized to make a point about homogeneous trends in labour earnings in different sectors throughout the developing world. The *WDR* would have done a great service in pointing to the existence of such material and the need for systematic analysis on a world-wide scale.

To my knowledge, no attempt is currently being made by any international agency, nor by their regional offices, to track the trends in labour market variables in the way suggested. The *Yearbook of Labour Statistics* is the most important regular publication of the ILO, but the bulk of the data presented in this voluminous publication refers to the formal sector. There is a companion publication that collects and reports the statistics on wages and earnings in selected occupations in a large number of countries. Theoretically, it provides the possibility to study the changes in earnings differentials by skill, occupation and industry, over time. But little guidance has been given to the National Statistical Offices for the coverage of the labour market on which they have been reporting, and it seems that most of the material again refers to the formal sector. Furthermore, in the absence of adequate resources provided to the ILO Statistical Department, it is not possible to monitor the returns closely, so that the dataset is marred by numerous missing values. As far as the World Bank is concerned, there has never been any attempt at a systematic collection of labour data in any of its departments.

It is no wonder that neither the *WDR* nor the ILO have provided much of a statistical annex to their respective reports on employment. The *WDR* has not added any new tables to their standard collection of *World Development Indicators* available in other years.[3]

Given this situation after so many years of data-gathering, by the ILO in particular, it is regrettable that neither of the two reports drew attention to this remarkable information gap.

E. Policy implications and country experience

We now turn to a critical evaluation of some of the major policy conclusions which the *WDR* draws from its review of world trends in employment and wages.

1. Growth strategy

While economic growth is diagnosed in the *WDR* to be the dominant factor in the improvement of workers' standard of living, it goes on to outline its evaluation of what is (or has been) a successful growth strategy. It distinguishes between "three patterns" of economic growth (p. 13): (a) the East Asian pattern with "a strong export orientation (which) reduced economic rents and a labor policy (which) did not favor privileged groups of workers"; (b) the inward-oriented development strategy, allegedly "pursued to varying degrees" by most countries in sub-Saharan Africa, Latin America, the Middle East, and South Asia, which "benefited a limited number of 'insiders', capital holders and workers employed in the protected sector"; and (c) the centrally planned economies which "were for decades exemplars of an economic model antithetical to the market model of the high-income industrial countries". The *Report* singles out the strategy of East Asia as being so much superior for ensuring sustained growth in incomes and wages.

It will be seen that the *Report* implicitly assumes that several different elements of economic policy are bound together in the "strategy" pursued. Although this might have been true for some countries' export orientation, non-participation of the State in economic enterprise and labour regulation favouring protected workers are logically and empirically separate packages of policy. Their relative importance in affecting the growth rate would be very different in different economies and indeed might not be in the same direction at all.

The weakest link in the chain of associated policies suggested is labour regulation. We have seen above that to suggest that labour market dualism is created by labour legislation is probably incorrect in most situations. In any event, labour regulation, if significant, is often secondary to other regulatory policies, for example, those affecting capital and product markets, and does not exist independently of them. There is no evidence given in the *WDR* that the East Asian strategy "mostly avoided sharp divides between modern sector and rural workers" (p. 13). Our own research suggests that the intersectoral differentials in earnings are of similar magnitudes in India and Indonesia.

As far as the role of the State is concerned, a distinction has to be made between the State as a direct producer of goods and services, on the one hand, and guiding economic policies of the Government, on the other. There is ample empirical evidence to suggest

that the State is a grossly inefficient producer. However, it is debatable if the role of the state in guiding the private economic agents was less important in East Asia than in South Asia. East Asian Governments in general seem to have created rents for entrepreneurs through direct subsidies, while South Asia created rents through import-substitution policies. The two forms of rent creation had quite different effects on growth rates because of the different orientation and effectiveness of State policies.

Export promotion was certainly an element in the distinctive policy orientation of several East Asian countries, even though in most cases there was a period of import-substitution strategy to lay the foundations for industrialization.[4] But it is not clear if it was the search for markets abroad per se rather than openness to foreign technology which was the major mover of the economic dynamics. We shall further discuss the relationship of exports to growth in section II. Here it is sufficient to make the point that, except in small economies, export growth by itself would not have a sustained upward impact on wages in different sectors of the economy. In his masterly analysis of economic growth in the "golden age" of non-European growth, 1870-1913, Arthur Lewis contrasts the differential impact of trade on the standard of living of the temperate countries and the tropics. The rate of growth of trade, mainly in primary commodities, from the tropics was nearly as high as from the countries of recent settlement, and both almost equalled the rate of growth in trade of the "core" industrial countries. Yet the standard of living of workers was much higher in the temperate countries than in the tropics and increased over time relative to that in the latter (Arthur Lewis, 1978, chapters 7 and 8). This was because the supply price of labour, reflecting the level of productivity in food production, was much higher in the temperate countries, and continued to increase over time relative to the levels in the tropics. "The tropics were held back by their need for a technological revolution in agriculture such as has been occurring in Western Europe over two centuries [which supplied labour to the temperate regions]" (Arthur Lewis, 1978, p. 202; phrase in parentheses not in the original). The essential point is that when a large portion of the labour force is employed in food production, it is the productivity in this sector which sets the supply price of labour to the rest of the economy, and unless exports are large relative to GDP, wages in the economy will not increase, except in some enclave sectors, unless the supply price increases through an increase in food productivity. Given the importance of the agricultural sector in wage growth, it is unfortunate that the *WDR* devoted only a limited amount of space to policies affecting agriculture.

2. *Agricultural policy*

The *WDR* does discuss agricultural policies in the section on "policy mistakes" (chapter 4, pp. 33-34), but the examples cited are made to support a polemical point that import-substituting regimes suffered from a pro-industry and anti-agriculture bias. Both South and East Asia, for example, supported agriculture through price support for farm products and subsidization of inputs. It is not clear that the net impact of policies was more adverse in South Asia.

The major difference between the two regions probably lies in the effectiveness of technological progress in food production. The *WDR* rightly draws attention to the importance of the "green revolution" in raising labour incomes, but the reasons for the slow development of this revolution in some parts of the developing world, including South Asia, are not adequately discussed. The reader is left with the misleading suggestion that a pro-industry bias was responsible for this relative stagnation in all regions.[5]

The report rightly stresses the peculiar situation in the agricultural sector of most developing regions in which production and technological progress has been hampered by the coexistence of small farms with a pressure of labour on land, and large farms with a significantly low labour-land ratio. This phenomenon has its origin in the unequal distribution of land. It is not rectified by large farms either hiring more labour, or leasing their land to the smaller farmers, to the extent required to attain similar levels of a man-land ratio on different size classes of farms. This is due to the imperfect working of interrelated factor markets for land, capital and labour.[6] Thus the marginal product of land and labour are at widely different levels in large and small farms leading to productive inefficiency. This phenomenon is particularly serious in Latin America, and cries out for intervention on both equity and efficiency grounds. The first-best solution is redistribution of land through land reform. The *WDR* seems to recognize this but spends little space and time commenting on the enormous problems of political economy which this entails. Nor is the success, and to some extent the political luck, of East Asia in going some way towards the redistributive solution stressed. In the absence of the first-best solution, strong intervention in favour of small farmers is called for to address this serious problem of the agricultural sector. But all too often political will and resources are lacking.

The problem has worsened in large parts of the developing world in the last 15 years or so. In Latin America, agricultural GDP fell in 11 of the 19 countries in the 1980s. This can hardly be associated with import-substitution policies which had largely been abandoned during the decade. Along with the falling rural incomes, "there was also an increasing share of employment in the traditional agricultural sector accompanied by falling average farm sizes, increased landlessness and falling real wages" (ILO, 1995, p. 94).

A serious deficiency of the *WDR* is its very limited treatment of African issues. This is also reflected in the discussion of African agricultural policies: "Much of this inequality [between rural and urban incomes] has its origins in decades of policies that favoured cities over the countryside. While in many countries these have been partly or fully abandoned, in others, especially in Africa, they remain in place" (*WDR*, p. 45). Very few serious analysts would treat this diagnosis as a helpful contribution to Africa's massive agricultural problem today. The ILO estimates that during 1987-1991 the median growth rate of food production per economically active population was -8 per cent, while that of agricultural exports -20 per cent. This was in the period in which various structural adjustment policies had significantly improved the terms of trade in favour of agriculture. The ILO employment report is much more on the right track in suggesting that the failure of African farmers to respond to improved price incentives is partly due to "the termination of subsidized sales of inputs and distribution programmes ... state credit programmes have also been cut back and private credit has not yet moved in to fill the void ... In addition, fiscal pressures, brought about by the economic decline and the reform process itself, have led to reductions in public investment in infrastructure" (ILO, 1995, p. 94).

In sum, the image of the predatory State taxing agriculture mercilessly can be overdone. Sustained public intervention in favour of the small farmers is almost certainly a prerequisite of agricultural growth. If, in some cases, policies have had perverse effects on the small farm sector, the correct line of approach is to expose the political economy of the particular States which permitted such abuse.

3. *The informal sector*

The analysis and policy conclusions about the informal sector in the *WDR* can be considered to be generally weak. There are many comments on the sector scattered throughout the *Report*, and some of them, for example those referring to informal arrangements for labour standards in the sector, are quite perceptive. But one looks in vain for a clear statement of possible approaches to helping the sector. This is unfortunate, given the enormous importance of the sector in the developing countries.

Perhaps the *WDR* position is that the informal sector is really a product of economic backwardness, and will "shrink with development" (figure 4.3, p. 45). There can be no doubt that a significant part of employment in the sector is a direct result of low incomes and low rates of growth in the economy. The demand for some of the goods and services produced by the sector comes from poor households and has a low-income elasticity. On the supply side, the informal sector serves as a "sponge" for the growing labour force which cannot find productive employment either in agriculture or in the formal sector. The poor economic performance of Latin America and Africa in the 1980s seems to have led to a large increase in the size of this sector.

There is, however, another part of the informal sector which does not consist of dead-end survival activities, but where there is considerable potential for growth and technical upgrading. Government policies need to be oriented towards encouraging this sector. This approach could be justified both on efficiency and equity grounds. We have already argued in the discussion above that distortions in factor markets, more so in capital than in labour markets, lead to a bias against small-scale enterprises in many economies. Support for such units through appropriate policies which compensate for these distortions would increase overall efficiency. It would also result in a more equitable distribution of both entrepreneurial and labour incomes. In this context the contrast between Taiwan Province of China and the Republic of Korea as models of development within the East Asian experience of export-oriented growth is of particular importance. The Republic of Korea opted for a package of policies which encouraged large-scale enterprises with the aim of exploiting economies of scale. Policies in Taiwan Province of China were much more oriented to the development of small- and medium-sized enterprises through innovative institutions which provided venture capital as well as technical help to small entrepreneurs. Taiwan Province of China achieved as successful a record of GDP growth as the Republic of Korea, and at the same time has been able to avoid the problems of overcentralization and concentration which have been plaguing the Republic of Korea in recent years.

While help with credit and technical know-how occupy the pride of place in the package of policies to support the small-scale sector, there are other areas which require the attention of Governments. In many economies, regulations often work against this sector. It has been reported by de Soto (1989) that the acquisition of a license to operate a street kiosk takes a month and a half and costs five times the minimum monthly wage. The illegal activities which such regulations encourage hamper the healthy growth of the informal economy. Infrastructural facilities such as power, telecommunications, water and transport, are typically biased against the sector. Urban land policies often fail to provide adequate property rights to settlements of the poor, making it impossible for them to produce titles to assets which might be used for collateral purposes.

II. Globalization and the growth of labour incomes

Part II of the *World Development Report 1995* is devoted to the demonstration of the increased globalization of national economies through a massive increase in international trade and factor movements, and the implications of this development for labour incomes in both the "North" and the "South". In some ways this topic is given the centre stage as the subtitle of the report "Workers in an Integrating World" suggests. The ILO's employment report similarly starts off right in its Chapter 1 with a detailed analysis of "Globalization and Employment". The treatment of the issues in both documents is masterly. The authors of the two reports are to be congratulated in bringing to the focus of public discussion a variety of issues which will be closely watched in the coming years. It is not easy to range over this wide canvas and pinpoint the most important points in a short space. Inevitably there will be disagreement on the emphasis and conclusions, not the least because the relevant issues are continuously evolving. It is not possible to have a comprehensive discussion of all topics in this short essay; in the following, a number of issues which appear to be the most controversial will be discussed selectively.

A. *Expansion of trade*

The *WDR* starts with a very useful demonstration of the dramatic fall in transport and communication costs since 1920, and the reduction in barriers to trade which have fuelled the massive increase in world trade since the Second World War. This recognition of fast growth in trade is not new. It has been in the concern of observers and a large number of policy makers in developing countries for at least 25 years. But there has also been a long-term concern about the ability of the world economy to sustain this high growth rate of trade without serious periodic disruptions (as, for example, after the oil crisis of 1973). In his famous Nobel Lecture of 1980, Arthur Lewis had the following to say about trade as an "engine of growth":

> The extraordinary growth rates of the two decades before 1973 surprised everybody. We know that the world economy experienced long swings in activity; that world trade, for example, grew faster between 1830 and 1873 than it grew between 1873 and 1913, that is to say between 4 and 5 per cent before 1873, compared with between 3 and 4 per cent after 1873. But a jump to 8 per cent was inconceivable ... The fact that world trade was growing rapidly was not recognized until the second half of the 1960s. Then nearly every country discovered the virtues of exporting. Now we are in danger of being caught out again. Since 1973 the growth rate of world trade has halved and nobody knows whether this is temporary or permanent (Arthur Lewis, 1980, pp. 555-556).

As it turned out, the interruption after the oil shock was indeed temporary. After a decade of slow growth between 1974 and 1983, the rate of growth of the volume of trade recovered to 6.4 per cent p.a. in the second half of the 1980s. But in the 1990s, the growth rate has slowed down again, to around 4 per cent. It is expected that further trade liberalization through the Uruguay Round and other measures would restore the growth rate to the higher trend level of the 1960s and 1970s. But against this much vaunted prediction is the spectre of prolonged recession in OECD economies. These remarks are not meant to revive fears of the "slowing down of the engine of growth", but only to guard against the undiluted optimism of both the *WDR* and the ILO report.

In any event, it is rather odd for commentators to talk about globalization as a strangely new phenomenon of the contemporary economic world. The growth rate of world trade has no doubt been unprecedented (barring the bouts of slow down) since the Second World War. But so has been the growth rate of GDP, and to some extent the rates of growth observed in this period are recoveries to earlier levels interrupted by the disruptions ushered in by the First World War. Pritchett (1995) reports that the ratio of exports to GDP for 17 developed countries for which historical data are available was twice as high in 1991 as in 1950, but only one and a half percentage points higher in 1993 than in 1913.

B. Changes in the pattern of trade

A point of greater concern which can be demonstrated with existing facts is the imbalance in the growth of trade affecting the developing world. There has indeed been a break in the traditional dependence of developing country trade on primary commodities. The developing countries' share of manufactured exports to the developed countries increased from 5 to 14 per cent between 1970 and 1990.[7] This is all to the good, but the less optimistic side of the picture is that much of this growth is really due to the growth in one region, primarily the East and South-East Asian economies and China. In Asia as a whole, manufactured exports in 1990 accounted for as much as 65.5 per cent of total exports, only around 12 percentage points below the share of manufactures in the exports of developed countries. But in spite of the increase of manufactures in their exports, Africa and Latin America remain predominantly exporters of primary commodities.

A major critique of world trade in the context of North-South development issues was the classic statement made by Nurkse (1959) in his Wicksell lectures. The essence of the argument was that world trade was dominated by the exchange of goods among the developed countries. The flow of trade thus by-passed the developing countries. In terms of its quantitative significance, trade could indeed be a handmaiden of growth for the developed countries, but could scarcely have a major impact on growth in the developing world.[8] Has the pattern changed in the phase of rapid expansion of trade in recent decades? The ILO report provides the answer, unfortunately in the negative:

> The share of Asian developing countries increased from 4.6 to 12.5 per cent between 1970 and 1991, but those of Latin America and sub-Saharan Africa fell. The overall developing country share increased only slightly as a result of this divergence in performance. Over the same period the share of the former socialist countries fell from 10 to 5 per cent. The upshot is that the share of the developed market economies remained unchanged at 71 per cent. Thus the major shift was a redistribution among the non-industrialized countries, with Asia gaining relative to the rest. (ILO, 1995, p. 32).

The *WDR* has at many points recognized that the "golden age of trade expansion" has largely benefited the East and South-East Asian regions disproportionately in the developing world. But it would have been appropriate to devote more attention to the trade-related problems of Africa and Latin America. In particular, the deterioration in recent years of the conditions of trade in primary commodities, which as we saw are still critical to the performance of Africa and Latin America, regrettably have not been discussed very much.

This is not the place to discuss this important set of issues in any detail. Excellent reviews exist, including one in this series (Maizels, 1995). Maizels points out that "a dramatic change occurred at the beginning of the 1980s in the international markets for non-oil primary commodities. Whereas the dominant feature in previous post-war decades had been abnormally short-term price fluctuations for a wide range of commodities, as from the early 1980s the dominant feature has been the persistence of exceptionally depressed price levels for a relatively prolonged period" (p. 82). Real commodity prices, that is, the ratio of nominal price indices for commodities and manufactures, declined at an annual rate of -3.3 per cent between 1979-1981 and 1983-1985 and at the rate of -5.4 per cent between 1983-1985 and 1989-1991. Maizels calculated that on "a cumulative basis, the loss over the whole period was equivalent to over 2.5 times the value of all non-oil commodity exports from developing countries in 1980" (p. 85). Factors on both the demand and supply side of the equation seem to have been responsible for this massive loss. They include the slowdown in the OECD growth rate and a sharp reduction in the raw material content of industrial production on the demand side; and farm support programmes in temperate-zone agriculture and the pressures of structural adjustment programmes on the supply side. Furthermore, the trends are seen to be more serious when we take account of regional disparities. In terms of purchasing power over manufactured imports, sub-Saharan Africa fared the worst with a massive decline of 35 per cent during 1980-1991. The decline in Latin America was 14 per cent, while Asia seems to have had an improvement of the index by about 8 per cent. (Maizels, 1995, table 2). The loss in terms of commodity trade has fallen disproportionately on the poorest region of the world, the region which has also seen the least diversification of exports into non-primary products.

The *WDR* does devote a sentence or two to this major issue in the evolution of world trade in a short section on "countries left behind" (p. 60). But given the seriousness of the problem and the long discussion in the development literature of the many complex issues in commodity trade, the throwaway suggestion that "most sub-Saharan commodity exporters were not able to keep up with the competition", seems singularly hollow and inadequate. It is worth noting that the ILO report also says next to nothing about commodity trade in its long chapter on globalization and employment.

One cannot help concluding that in both reports globalization has been implicitly associated with the increase in manufacturing trade, foreign direct investment and the activities of multinational corporations. These are the more recent phenomena, and they have dominated the attention of the authors of the two reports. But globalization, in a more basic sense, has been present for a century or more, ever since the countries of the "periphery" were opened up to trade by the developed countries. The welfare of primary producers has been tied to the fortunes of the developed economies for all this time. By focusing too much on manufacturing, both the *WDR* and the ILO report have neglected the older problems of trade in primary products which continue to be of major importance.

C.　*Export growth and wage increase*

The *WDR* makes a big point about the virtues of increase in trade in augmenting labour incomes. In so far as the growth of exports increases the demand for labour, its potential impact on labour incomes, both for wage earners and the self-employed, is clear. There are other indirect effects which are instrumental in raising incomes in the economy as a whole, and often labour shares the benefits of growth. The *WDR* message will be acceptable in large parts; very few policy makers will disagree with the main thrust of the argument. After all, as the quotation from the Lewis Nobel lecture given above shows, this message had been accepted in place of the import-substitution and autarchic paradigm of the 1950s quite some time ago. The development of South-East Asian countries round the growth pole of East Asia, and the collapse of the former closed socialist economies, have given a new lease on life to the export-orientation message. But it is unfortunate that the argument is sometimes bolstered with forced empirical illustrations which can only detract from the value of the message. An example is the supposed statistical proof of the rise in real wages with export intensity (export-to-GNP ratio) in figure 8.1 (WDR, p. 55). The statistical association, which does not appear to be particularly strong, cannot be used to support any causal relationship. Observations on real wages in formal manufacturing are related to the economy-wide export/GNP ratio; and the mixing of small and large economies in the scatter gives the exercise an air of polemic. The *WDR* might have been well advised to note some of the cautionary points about the impact of export growth on labour incomes.

First, the pattern of trade matters. The issue of trade in primary products and terms of trade loss have already been discussed. Secondly, even within manufacturing, overexpansion in exports can lead to welfare loss, especially if it is achieved with directed subsidies and deliberate devaluation. The domestic economy could be, and in some countries has been, severely taxed to support export expansion. Thirdly, it is worth repeating that, except in small open economies, the demand impact of export growth is not sufficient in achieving an economy-wide increase in labour incomes. It is important to increase the supply price of labour by increasing productivity in the sectors in which much labour is engaged, especially in food production. We could cite the example of a large economy within the much-vaunted South-East Asian economies - Indonesia. The green revolution ushered in by intelligent use of oil revenues in infrastructure investment and seed-fertilizer price subsidies was instrumental in raising farm incomes and labour earnings in other sectors. This development preceded the export growth of the late 1980s.

D.   Trade and inequality

A major concern of recent discussions on the impact of globalization is inequality in the distribution of labour incomes. Discussions have all focused on the development of new technology in industry with its requirement for more skilled labour. There are at least three distinct topics in this area: (i) The impact on earnings inequality in the developed countries resulting from the relocation of industry on the basis of the worldwide distribution of skilled labour; (ii) the regional distribution of "good jobs" within the third world; and (iii) the impact of liberalization and increased trade in manufactures on earnings inequality in the exporting developing countries. These issues are of topical concern. The *WDR* rightly devotes a good deal of attention to them, as does the ILO report, but the style of treatment in the two reports differs.

The *WDR* is probably more accessible in its discussion of these topics. The ILO report devotes more space to them in an analytical way, but at the same time its frequent reference to the academic literature makes the chapter heavy going.

The authors of both reports are to be congratulated on taking the trouble to digest the evolving literature on complex issues and bringing the issues to public attention. The comments that follow are not meant to detract from the major contributions made; they should be regarded as supplementary points which we believe need to be emphasized.

1.   The impact on the developed countries

The empirical facts are clear: there has been a sharp increase in the last decade in the earnings of skilled workers relative to those of unskilled workers in the USA and many OECD countries. Most indices of earnings inequality have shown an upward trend after many decades of narrowing differentials. The diagnosis of these trends is, however, not yet clear. The controversy ranges round the relative importance of trade and technological change in causing these trends. On the one hand, there has been some work done suggesting that the most profitable location for labour-intensive manufactured goods has shifted to the newly industrializing countries of the South, such that the North is increasing its imports of these goods at the cost of reduction of its own manufacturing employment. The alternative hypothesis highlights the importance of the new technology, particularly that based on information and communications technology, which is "skill-intensive". The spread of this revolution, which is likely to gather speed in the immediate future, has allegedly led to a fall in the labour-output ratio in manufacturing, and further to the exclusion of large groups of workers who are unskilled or not readily trainable in the new technology. Empirical evidence based on partial analysis has been produced to support both the hypotheses.[9] Probably there is an element of truth in both. Some qualifications, however, need to be made on the impact of trade on unskilled employment in the North even if there is a significant negative effect.

First, manufactured imports from developing countries still account for only 14 per cent of the total manufactured imports of OECD countries (OECD, 1993; the figure is for 1992).

Secondly, one must take into account the feedback of Southern growth on the North. The exports of the North to the South increase with faster growth in the South. The consumers gain in the North. The multinational corporations in the North gain from enlarged investment opportunities in the South. Thus, a possible short-term negative effect on northern employment must not detract from the strong long-term gains. The *WDR* very rightly comes out with a strong position against protectionist sentiments in the United States and other OECD countries. In particular, it warns against the strategy of protection taking the form of demands for "adequate" labour standards in Southern manufacturing. This point is discussed further in connection with the general issues of labour regulation in the next section.

2. The regional distribution of manufacturing in the South

The second major issue in trade expansion is concerned with regional inequality in the benefits of trade within the South. We come back to the point already made in subsection B above that the growth in manufacturing exports has been regionally concentrated in East and South-East Asia. Employment in manufacturing creates "good" jobs with higher wages, and it leads to skill acquisition which pushes upwards lifetime wage profiles. Traditionally, expansion of the share of employment in manufacturing has been seen in the development literature as the way economies would shed surplus labour and increase labour incomes. The East Asian countries have indeed done so. Expansion of manufactured exports in these economies has been closely associated with the increase in the share of employment in manufacturing. But why has this development been most marked in East and South-East Asia so far? Inadequate trade and macroeconomic policies, as well as political instability, have often been pointed out as being responsible for the relative stagnation of manufacturing in South Asia, Latin America and Africa. The *WDR* has repeated the traditional explanations. Recently, Adrian Wood (1994a and 1994b) has gelled together into a coherent model some concerns about a more fundamental economic reason for these regional differences. This line of reasoning gives a somewhat different slant to policy options than what has been advocated in the *WDR*. Interestingly, the *WDR* reproduces the empirical basis of Wood's model (Box 8.2, p. 59) but stops short of drawing or even discussing the implications of the model.

Briefly, Wood modifies the Heckscher-Ohlin (H-O) model of factor proportions in the country defining its comparative advantage in trade, by simply reconsidering the key factors of production which help to determine comparative advantage. In particular, Wood differentiates labour into skilled and unskilled labour and assumes that their relative stocks differ from country to country and are not that easy to change in the short run. The reasons for this key assumption will be given shortly.[10] Comparative advantage in manufactures is determined not so much by the ratio of capital to labour as in the classical H-O model (capital is indeed internationally mobile today, unlike in the H-O world) but by the ratio of the country's stock of skilled labour to that of its natural resources. Unskilled labour, without any formal education or training, is not suitable for the formal (large-scale) manufacturing sector. Skilled labour, of course, varies in levels of training, and the degree of skill can be approximated by the average years of education. Wood measures the skill intensity of a country by the ratio of average years of education per adult population (above 25) to the amount of land per adult. Taking a cross-section of 114 countries with a population of more than a million, Wood obtained a significant relationship between the ratio of manufactured to primary exports and the skill ratio. The regression accounted for 57 per cent of the variance. The same strong relationship is found when, instead of individual countries, six regions of the world are used as units of observation.[11] Wood takes this rather striking result to justify his hypothesis about the skill intensity of the labour force determining the comparative advantage in manufacturing.

The *WDR* reproduces the graphical presentation of this regression, but seeks to draw different conclusions than Wood. It writes: "Although [the scatter diagram] was estimated on the basis of cross-sectional data for 1985, it can also be used to determine the dynamics of development. Progress in the diagram consists of a movement upward to the right." That is to say, the implication is that countries gradually increase their skill intensity with human capital accumulation and improve their comparative advantage in manufactures.

Wood, on the other hand, is concerned with the implication for manufactured exports of the differences between the different regions of the world in skill intensity, as it exists today. The East Asian experience is one of employment creation in high-wage sectors through rapid expansion in manufactured exports. Its replicability is severely limited by the low-skill intensity of other regions. The closest to East Asia is South Asia, but even here the skill intensity ratio as measured is only one quarter of the ratio in the high performers of East Asia. Latin

America and the Caribbean have a skill ratio of one eighth of the East Asian high performers, while sub-Saharan Africa reveals extreme deprivation with a skill ratio of only 4 per cent of the level of the latter. If Wood's hypothesis is correct then the chances of development of manufactured exports, in a significant way in the near future, is low in Latin America and almost negligible in Africa.

To close the argument, Wood needs to establish that it is difficult for low-skill countries to travel swiftly up the skill ladder. He has done a great service to the debate by showing that the quantitative gap between regions in skill intensity is enormous. It has probably increased in the recent decade of structural adjustment with the slashing of public spending for education. But the quality and contents of education also matter. We know too little about the speed with which the stock of relevant skills can, or even has been in the past, augmented. *WDR's* chapter 5 on human capital is not helpful in the absence of specific research on the nature of skill accumulation. One suggestion for research would be a comparison of the evolution of the education and training systems in the successful countries of East Asia with the laggards in other parts of Asia. Wood merely makes the point that "skill acquisition is at best a slow process for a country, largely because each person's learning depends on the skills of those around them (parents, teachers, colleagues)" (Wood, 1994a, p. 24).

He also draws attention to the perverse effect of international migration, in which highly skilled labour migrates from low-skill to high-skill countries, an effect which Wood ascribes to the external economies of "clustering" of skilled labour. Finally, he suggests that the classical "infant industry protection" theory had a substantial message, verified by history, about the use of protection from external competition of specific industries, as one of the instruments for raising skill levels in the economy. The fact that imperfect States have abused the power of trade restriction, at great cost to the welfare of their population, does not destroy the validity of the point.

3.   Impact of trade expansion on inequality in developing countries

In the last decade a number of developing countries have pushed through important measures of liberalization of trade and other areas of their economies. The *WDR* recognizes that many of these measures have led to a deterioration in the distribution of income. The upheaval in economic institutions and restructuring has, of course, led to large increases in

unemployment and falling real wages in the formerly socialist countries, and also in many African economies. Even in Latin America where redeployment of labour across sectors and the decline in GDP have been moderate (*WDR*, p. 99), the "poor certainly suffered during the macro-economic crisis" (p. 104). But the *WDR* position is that this result "was a product of past policy mistakes and not a consequence of adjustment policies *per se*". After referring to divergent movements in the indices of inequality in different countries of Latin America, it remarks: "For the region as a whole, trends in inequality appear more closely tied to the economic cycle than to reform, with income inequality and poverty rising during recessions and falling after recovery" (p. 104).

This result was based on the data of the 1980s. The hope expressed was that the renewal of growth following adjustment would lead to a reduction in inequality and poverty. More recent research, still not formally published, casts serious doubt on this optimistic assessment.[12]

The focus of that study is on the impact of economic reforms, principally liberalization measures, on distribution. Thus, the empirical evidence has been based on observations, from household surveys, at points before and after the whole crisis-stabilization-adjustment sequence. Countries differed in the time period when the reforms were undertaken. "In Argentina, Chile and Uruguay, the main events occurred in the 1970s; in Mexico and the Dominican Republic in the 1980s, and in Colombia, Ecuador, Peru and Brazil at the end of the 1980s and the early 1990s" (Berry, 1995, pp. 56-57). The methodology thus differs from that underlying Figure 16.1 of the *WDR*, which considers only the period from 1980 to 1991.

The main results are summarized by Berry as follows:

> The country experiences reviewed above suggest that the "normal" observed increase in inequality accompanying reforms is 5-10 percentage points as measured by the Gini-coefficient of primary income ... It seems likely that this increase is typically the result of a jump in the share of the top decile, most of this accruing to the top 5 per cent or perhaps the top 1 per cent (as in the case of Colombia and Ecuador, households) while most of the bottom deciles lose ... In Ecuador where the percentage decline for the bottom decile was sharper (from 2.2 per cent to 1.5

per cent), nearly 20 years of distribution-neutral growth at 2 per cent per capita would be needed and about eight years at 5 per cent (to recover the lost ground) (Berry, p. 55).

Trade liberalization seems to shift the price vector in favour of higher-income families, primarily because the comparative advantage of the region does not lie in unskilled-labour-intensives products. In terms of the Wood model discussed earlier, if liberalization encourages mostly industrial exports, it is the more skilled workers who would benefit. The process is encouraged by foreign investment and the associated transfer of new skill-intensive technology. Although the optimistic expectation was that opening-up of trade would increase the relative income of agricultural workers, a significant part of the increase in income inequality has been due to the widening gap between rural and urban incomes, particularly in Mexico and Colombia. "It is clear that in such countries there is a major part of the agricultural sector which cannot compete with an onslaught of imports, and whose labor resources are unlikely to be quickly mobile to other sectors" (Berry, pp. 57-58).

Similar warning signals about the adverse distributional effects of liberalization have come from other regions of the world as well. The ILO employment report warns that, "in India, concern has been expressed over the likely impact of the New Economic Policy on agricultural development ... If these changes are introduced then, together with improved incentives to agribusiness as a result of liberalization, they could well undermine the survival of small farms".

These warnings are not meant to detract from the growth-oriented liberalization programmes, but only to make policy makers aware of emerging problems which need to be closely monitored and analysed. The *WDR* could well have drawn attention to these important concerns.

III. Labour regulation

Part III of the *WDR* deals with institutions which have a regulatory or interventionist impact on labour markets. These include government legislation directed to labour matters; unions and their role; and the public sector as a direct employer. We start the discussion with legislation, but reference to workers' organizations and the public sector will inevitably come into the discussion at appropriate points.

A. *Principles of regulation: equity and efficiency*

The *WDR* discussion begins with an analysis of the principles which underlie the logic of labour market intervention. These include uneven market power which tilts the balance of the outcome in favour of capital owners in the absence of intervention; discrimination against particular groups of workers; imperfect information on the part of employees, as well as many employers, about the work environment, particularly that relating to safety and health standards; and lastly, the inadequate finance available to workers to adequately insure against unemployment, disability and old age. The *WDR* points out that in most of these cases intervention could be justified both on efficiency and equity grounds (p. 70). Intervention, however, need not be necessarily or primarily by the State.

The *WDR* rightly points out that in the rural and informal sectors which account for the vast majority of workers in many developing countries, numerous social arrangements exist for controlling labour market outcomes. But it is somewhat naively optimistic in suggesting that "such informal arrangements are by far the most important type of solutions to labour market problems" (p. 70, para. 6). Some types of informal institutions are clearly beneficial to workers, for example the extended family taking over much of the burden of insurance against sickness and old age; the downward rigidity of wage rates during the lean season; and the customary attempts of some transfers to the poorest sections through consumption supplements during social and religious occasions. But other forms of social arrangements are detrimental to both equity and efficiency, for example, discrimination by caste, ethnicity or gender. In this way, a society, through its informal institutions, acts in much the same way as the State. Sometimes they both act with welfare augmenting intentions, but at other times they can be instrumental in pursuing obvious policies detrimental to welfare.

For a meaningful discussion of labour market policies, we must assume that the intentions of government action are not deliberately welfare reducing. Only then can we consider the question whether particular types of action are successful in increasing welfare.

The first point to note about government action affecting labour markets is that in a developing country most measures can be enforced only in a narrow segment of the market, viz. the formal sector. Much of the *WDR* discussion turns on the legitimate concern that administrative costs are simply prohibitive in any attempt to impose labour legislation on a large number of small enterprises, and, of course they just do not apply to the self-employed sector. If we assume the general prevalence of competitive labour markets, then the imposition of labour legislation on a narrow segment would be detrimental to both equity and efficiency goals. Any attempt to increase the share of labour in output, for example, through legislation imposing minimum wages or non-wage benefits, would merely increase the welfare of a small segment of the labour force that are already earning a higher wage, and would also reduce growth in employment in this sector. The predictions of the simple competitive model are clear. The *WDR* does make some qualifications to such predictions, but the exceptions to the simple model could have been presented more effectively. The two principal exceptions are the prevalence of monopsony and considerations of external economies in labour markets.

1. Monopsony in labour markets

(a) The formal sector

A monopsony situation exists in a labour market if the individual employer is faced with an inelastic supply of labour. The theory of institutional imposition of a wage above the competitive level is well known in such a labour market. Both employment and wages could increase provided the employer has been earning excess profits and is not threatened with bankruptcy by the imposition of the higher wage. This was indeed the situation when English economists first conceived of minimum wages in "sweated" industries during the industrial revolution. These industries typically made use of pockets of geographically immobile labour, often women workers or children, who had little alternative opportunities of employment, and were therefore in inelastic supply to the few employers operating in the localized labour markets.

How general is this situation in labour markets in developing countries? At first sight, it might appear that with a large pool of surplus labour available from the rural sector, industrial enterprises in the urban markets would generally be faced with an elastic supply of labour, as in the Lewis model, especially if there is a wage differential in favour of the urban areas to cover the costs of migration. But enterprises, making use of high-priced capital equipment, often tend to develop their own firm-specific, stable labour force. Individual firms within the formal sector may indeed be faced with an inelastic supply of committed

labour force, of firm-specific skills, even if untrained labour or temporary workers are in elastic supply. The high labour productivity attained in these firms, aided by capital and product market imperfections, would in many cases provide a rent to be shared with labour. This is indeed the reason why wages are established at a much higher level than alternative earnings in the rural or the informal sectors.

The real problem of establishing minimum wages in such labour markets is that technology, capital-intensity and labour productivity vary widely among enterprises even within the formal sector. Thus it is extremely difficult to determine the level of a uniform minimum wage which is high enough to capture a significant part of the rent for the workers, but not so high as to make a large number of low-productivity enterprises bankrupt. A related difficulty is that if a cut-off point is adopted (as is generally the case) based on employment size below which the minimum wage is not applicable, it provides a serious disincentive to entrepreneurs to grow beyond this size. Long-run growth in productivity might be hurt in this case with firms being unwilling to exploit economies of scale or of technological progress.

There is thus considerable merit to the *WDR* case that unions based on enterprises rather than economy or industry-wide unions should be the ideal organization for collective bargaining on wages (p. 84). The problem is often that low-productivity and small units with low wages, are often the ones where unions are absent. There might be a case for the State providing some leadership by encouraging tripartite wage negotiation by establishing wage boards. Wage boards are sensitive to the wide interfirm productivity differentials which typically exist in the industrial sector of developing countries.

(b) The rural and informal sectors

Studies of rural labour markets have surprisingly revealed that the dominant pattern of wage determination is based on local labour markets, often defined by the boundaries of the village. With the general prevalence of underemployment or surplus labour one might have expected that village wage rates would have shown some uniform level in the same district, with a strong mode at the wage rate reflecting a notion of subsistence. In fact, the intervillage variation in wage levels is large. Variation in the productivity of land explains a substantial part of the observed variation in wage rates for agricultural labour (see Mazumdar, 1989, for a selective survey of the literature). The localized village-based labour market is not due to costs of migration since large differences are often observed in adjacent villages. Rather, it is the consequence of strong social relationships prevailing within the village. This type of situation suggests that labour would be in inelastic supply within the village, and the labour market might resemble a monopsony situation particularly for the larger employers. Institutional intervention in wages might easily be successful in raising both wages and employment, with a larger share of the pie transferred to the workers. The analysis extends to the employment of wage labour in rural industries. Labour employed for wages in food processing, construction, brick-making, etc., found coexisting with agriculture in the village economy, is also generally drawn from a local pool. Such markets are often monopsonistic with excess rental income.

In our view the case for minimum wages is conceptually strong in these sectors of the labour market. The problem is the absence of organizations which can implement a feasible scheme of wage intervention. Organizations of agricultural labour are rare in the social conditions of the rural society. Minimum-wage legislation is difficult to define at a realistic level, and implementation is costly unless the administrative apparatus is supported by grass-root political or social organizations. The few cases of attempts at minimum wage determination, for example in some Indian States, have not been adequately studied in the *WDR* or elsewhere.

If minimum-wage legislation for rural workers is impracticable, the case for public-works programmes becomes stronger. The *WDR* treats the public-works strategy as being "particularly appropriate during recessions, when other job opportunities are unavailable" (p. 87). But the longer-term aspects of such programmes in increasing the demand for labour across localized labour markets, and breaking up monopsonistic arrangements, are as important. The *WDR* comments: "Low labor mobility makes these programs less effective - some studies have indicated that obstacles to mobility in China have made it more difficult for that country's public works programs to reach the poor" (p. 88). The difficulty, in fact, is the challenge.

2. External economies and labour market intervention

Intervention on wages or the conditions of work could sometimes be justified for the purposes of augmenting labour productivity. It is generally expected that a freely operating labour market would find the level of wages and associated working conditions which minimizes the cost of a standard unit of work. If this were the case, an increase in wages through intervention might increase efficiency somewhat, but the increase would be less than proportionate to the wage increase. It is, however, possible to conceive of situations in which entrepreneurs acting in a profit-maximizing way would be stuck in a labour market equilibrium with low wages and low productivity. This is because an individual employer acting on his own would, in the short run, incur higher wage cost if he increased wages. The labour system could be changed to a high-wage high-productivity one only if all employers were induced to act in unison, and nobody got penalized in the short run.

The point can be illustrated by the example of East and Southern African countries which inherited the migratory labour system in the urban labour market developed in the colonial era. The urban wage level was sufficient to attract only individual migrants who sought urban employment for short periods to supplement the farm income of their households. The very high rate of turnover which this wage policy induced led to low levels of skill retention and low productivity. A number of Commissions of Enquiry including the Royal Commission of Labour of 1954 reported that there was no chance of African labour attaining reasonable levels of skill and efficiency needed in modern industry, unless wage levels were raised to attract stable labour which only labour settled in town with their families could provide. It was not realistic to expect individual entrepreneurs to change the wage system, because the transition to a stable labour system would take time, and would work only if all or large numbers of employers increased the wage together to levels which would attract family migrants (Mazumdar, 1993). This was the basis of the large increases in minimum wages which took place in several African countries in the late 1950s and early 1960s. The wage increase had the desired effect in reducing labour turnover drastically. It is possible that the minimum-wage increase might have overshot its mark, but on the basis of the research available it cannot be said whether the productivity increase fell short of the wage increase.

For the present purposes it is sufficient to note that the principles of wage increase through intervention discussed above create a conflict between efficiency and equity, at least in the short run. The objective is to increase efficiency in modern industry, but it does so at the cost of reducing employment growth. With higher productivity and lower wage cost, the conflict might be reduced in the long run if industry becomes competitive and increases its rate of output growth.

Recent history of African labour markets have been quite different from that of the period of wage increase through minimum wages in the 1950s and 1960s. In the last two or three decades, African economies have witnessed a sustained fall in real wages in the urban formal sector (Mazumdar, 1994). Concerns have been expressed that in some economies wages might have fallen to levels which would again bring to the fore the problems of unstable labour and low efficiency. It might be argued that in the private sector recognition of efficiency wages would provide a floor to the fall in wages below which the wage cost of a unit of work increases. But when firms operate in a financially deteriorating environment and a reduction of real wages is induced by high rates of inflation, firms may not have the financial capacity to keep money wages chasing prices, even when they recognize the costs of real wage increase. The problem, of course, is much more serious in the public sector, where there is no objective way of measuring labour productivity, and the pressures to maintain employment are strong. Real wages could be, and most likely have been, allowed to fall to levels which inflate the real labour costs of public services. Since the supply of public services at reasonable costs is essential for economic growth, it is imperative that the short-run conflict between equity and efficiency be boldly recognized, and that Governments act to increase real wages. Similar situations may exist in other regions, though not as seriously as in Africa.

Recognition of external economies are important in a variety of possible interventions in labour markets, particularly those relating to the working conditions of weaker demographic groups. Two important examples relate to child labour and the conditions of employment of women.

The long discussion of policies for child labour in the *WDR* is very useful. However, it might have mentioned the important point that the restriction of child labour would surely have an important effect on shifting the emphasis from quantity to quality of children - by increasing the household cost per child - and on long-run economic growth. The question of enforcement, of course, remains, and so does the problem of the immediate costs to poor households. Historically, the provision of an effective education system, backed up by suitable legislation for compulsory schooling, has been the most successful method of controlling child labour in the West as well

as in East Asia. Parental cooperation might be sought through suitable schemes of education subsidies paid to poor households.

As far as women workers are concerned, their effectiveness and acceptability in the urban economy are much reduced by the lack of provision of maternity leave. It is very likely that the external economies associated with a successful implementation of maternity-leave provisions would be very high, given that there is a significant wage gap in favour of male workers in most economies. The crucial problem might be the impact of the costs associated with such legislation in the short run. One possibility is the help of trade unions or non-governmental organizations in the informal sector to sell the scheme to employers, as seems to have been done successfully in some urban areas in India.

IV. Conclusions

The *WDR* deals with a large number of issues in the area of employment. This review of the *WDR* might read as a sustained attack, but this is only because it has focused selectively on those topics which the author felt needed reassessment.

On policy issues, the *WDR* lumped together three elements which are logically and empirically separable: export orientation; minimum participation of the State in economic activities; and absence of labour regulations creating a privileged section of the labour force in the formal sector. In its most naive sections, the *WDR* seems to suggest that an ideal combination of these disparate elements constitutes the essence of the East Asian success story of development, which tends to be taken as a model for increasing labour incomes in the developing world.

This review has sought to provide a note of caution on the "export-orientated" strategy. The discussion draws attention to: (a) the exaggerated notions of the extent and recent increase in "globalization"; and (b) the major problems in the patterns of trade which continue to be important factors in the persistence of inequality. Too much attention on the few success stories of manufactured export growth in East Asian countries distracts from the serious traditional issues of trade in primary products, which are still dominant in the economies of Africa and Latin America. We believe that it is not unfair to criticize the *WDR* for a regional bias in its concerns and prescriptions.

In any event, except for small open economies, growth in the export sector is unlikely to be a sufficient or even major factor in the increase in labour incomes throughout the economy. What is needed are policies that increase the supply price of labour spilling out of the agricultural sector - and this could only be achieved by sustained increase in productivity in this sector. Hence the importance of government support for policies which increase technological progress and incomes in the small farm economy. Indonesia is a classic case of successful state policies which achieved this well before manufactured exports started to increase in the second half of the 1980s.

The identification in the *WDR* of active involvement of the State in economic development with import-substitution strategy is not helpful. First, the State has historically been an active agent in export promotion in the successful South Asian economies. Secondly, it distracts attention from the essential role of the State in the development of the small farm sector.

Similarly, holding labour legislation responsible for the creation of a privileged formal sector of workers is incorrect. In fact, intervention is often necessary to correct the inequity and inefficiency resulting from labour market segmentation caused by a variety of factors in developing economies.

The *WDR's* treatment of labour market segmentation and the informal sectors of the labour market are weak, partly because of the lack of a realistic model of the labour market in developing countries, and partly because of the large gap in available statistical information on the non-formal sectors. Time and again the *WDR* had to fall back on labour data pertaining to the formal sector, when the argument clearly needed attention to the facts of the non-formal economy. Given that the informal sector (including agriculture) is the dominant part of the labour market in most developing countries, more effort is clearly called for in the collection and organization of labour data for this part of the market. The misdirection of effort in international organizations, including the ILO and the World Bank, is partly responsible for this deficiency. Labour force surveys which include the informal sector have become increasingly common in the work of national statistical offices. But, at the international level, organizations responsible for disseminating information on labour matters have a long way to go to build on these efforts.

Notes

1 However, the World Bank has prepared a separate report, *Adjustment in Africa: Reforms, Results and the Road Ahead* (New York: Oxford University Press, 1994), a review of which has already been published in this series (Lipumba, 1995). The next *World Development Report* is scheduled to be on the problems of economies in transition.

2 Typically, wage labour in peasant agriculture is hired on daily contracts as required. Permanent year-round employment is only a small proportion of wage employment on family farms, and is more typical of plantations.

3 As far as the ILO is concerned, we were informed that a statistical appendix to the employment report had been planned, but the tables had so many gaps that it was finally decided not to publish them.

4 Most East Asian countries adopted import-substitution strategies in their initial phases of development after the Second World War. The Republic of Korea went through an import-substituting phase in the middle of its growth process as well. After the success of its export-oriented strategy with light industry, there was a deliberate attempt, following the first oil crisis, to lay the foundations for heavy industries for the future. An import-substitution strategy promoting such industries was pursued. Although criticized at the time, many scholars believe that these policies laid the foundation for the country's success in developing newer types of export industries in the 1980s.

5 It might seem ungracious to expect the *WDR* to discuss all questions adequately. But the food sector in which a large proportion of the labour force works surely deserves a chapter more than trade unions which are relevant only for a narrow segment of the labour market in most developing countries, and even then their importance is probably not very great.

6 For a fuller discussion of this phenomenon and its causes see Mazumdar (1989).

7 These and other figures in this paragraph are taken from ILO (1995), p. 33 (derived from UNCTAD, various years).

8 This idea, indeed, was one of the elements of the import-substitution strategy of development which dominated policy making in much of the third world in the 1950s and 1960s.

9 Some examples have been cited in the ILO report. For example, Sachs and Schatz (1994) calculate that imports from developing countries have caused a 6 per cent reduction in the demand for unskilled workers in manufacturing between 1978 and 1990. On the other hand, Lawrence and Slaughter (1993) suggest that if trade patterns have reduced the demand for unskilled labour, one would expect the ratio of unskilled to skilled labour to rise across the board in all industries as the latter adjust to the new composition of labour supply. But in the United States the opposite seems to have happened. There has been an across-the-board decrease in the ratio of unskilled to skilled labour. The forces from the demand side, transmitted by the technological revolution, has overshadowed the pressure from the supply side. OECD (1992) has provided an analysis of employment changes by industry, which shows that in the member countries the relatively small gains in high-technology industries have been overshadowed by falling in employment in others.

10   In fact, Wood considers three types of labour: unskilled workers with no schooling, more skilled workers with a basic general education, and highly skilled with professional or technical qualification. For our restricted purposes, it is not necessary to consider the distinction between the last two.

11   The six regions are: the developed countries; East Asia (total); East Asia (high performing); Latin America and the Caribbean; South Asia; and sub-Saharan Africa.

12   The research was carried out under the auspices of FOCAL (Canadian Foundation for the Americas) and executed by the Centre for International Studies, University of Toronto. The data used were household surveys carried out at discrete dates between the 1970s and the mid-1990s. The countries included are Argentina, Brazil, Chile, Colombia, Costa Rica, the Dominican Republic, Ecuador, Mexico and Uruguay. The account in the text is based on the overview by Berry (1995).

References

ARTHUR LEWIS, William (1978), *Growth and Fluctuations 1870-1913* (London: George Allen & Unwin).

ARTHUR LEWIS, William (1980), "The slowing down of the engine of growth", *American Economic Review*, Vol. 70, No. 4, pp. 555-564.

BERRY, Albert (1995), "The Social Challenge of the New Economic Era in Latin America", *Focal/CES Discussion Papers* (University of Toronto: Centre for International Studies).

DE SOTO, H. (1989), *The other path: The invisible revolution in the Third World* (New York: Harper and Row).

ILO (Various years), *Yearbook of Labour Statistics* (Geneva).

ILO (Various years), *Bulletin of Labour Statistics*, *Special supplement reporting the results of the 'October Survey'* (Geneva).

ILO (1995), *World Employment 1995* (Geneva).

LAWRENCE, Robert Z., and Matthew J. SLAUGHTER (1993), "International trade and American wages in the 1980s: Giant sucking sound or small hiccup?", *Brookings Papers on Economic Activity, Microeconomics*, Vol. 2.

LIPUMBA, Nguyuru H. I. (1995), "Structural Adjustment Policies and Economic Performance of African Countries", in UNCTAD, *International Monetary and Financial Issues for the 1990s*, Vol. V (UNCTAD/GID/G24/5)(New York and Geneva: United Nations), pp. 35-64.

MAIZELS, Alfred (1995), "The Functioning of International Markets for Primary Commodities: Key Policy Issues for Developing Countries", in UNCTAD, *International Monetary and Financial Issues for the 1990s*, Vol. V (UNCTAD/GID/G24/5)(New York and Geneva: United Nations), pp. 81-114.

MAZUMDAR, Dipak (1973), "Labour supply in early industrialization", *Economic History Review*, Vol. 20, No. 3, pp. 477-497.

MAZUMDAR, Dipak (1989), "Microeconomic Issues of Labor Markets in Developing Countries: Analysis and Policy Implications", *EDI Seminar Paper*, No. 40 (Washington, D.C.: Economic Development Institute of the World Bank).

MAZUMDAR, Dipak (1993), "Wages and Employment in Kenya", mimeo., World Bank, Africa Chief Economist's Office, Washington, D.C., June.

MAZUMDAR, Dipak (1994), "Wages in Africa", mimeo., World Bank, Africa Chief Economist's Office, Washington, D.C., February.

NURKSE, Ragnar (1959), *Patterns of Trade and Development* (Stockholm: Almquist and Wiksell).

OECD (1992), *Technology and the economy: The key relationships* (Paris).

PRITCHETT, L. (1995), "Capital Flows: Five Stylized Facts for the 1990s", paper presented at the meeting on "Managing economic reform under Capital flow volatility", 31 May.

SACHS, Jeffrey, and Howard J. SCHATZ (1994), "Trade and Jobs in US Manufacturing", *Brookings Papers on Economic Activity*, Vol. I, pp. 1-84.

SHINOHARA, Miyohei (1962), "Growth and Cycles in the Japanese Economy", *Economic Research Series*, No. 5 (Kunitachi: Hitosubashi University).

SUSSANKARN, C. (1989), "Labor Markets in an Era of Adjustment: A Study of Thailand", in S. Horton, R. Kanbur and D. Mazumdar, *Labor Markets in an Era of Structural Adjustment*, Volume II (Washington, D.C.: Economic Development Institute of the World Bank).

UNCTAD (various years), *Handbook of International Trade and Development Statistics* (New York and Geneva: United Nations).

WORLD BANK (1995), *World Development Report 1995. Workers in an Integrating World* (Washington, D.C.).

WOOD, Adrian (1994a), "Trade and Employment Creation: Possibilities and Limitations", paper presented at a Workshop on Development Strategy, OECD Development Centre, Paris, 11-13 July.

WOOD, Adrian (1994b), *North-South Trade, Employment and Inequality: Changing Fortunes in a Skill-driven World* (Oxford: Clarendon Press).

THE URUGUAY ROUND - COSTS AND COMPENSATION FOR DEVELOPING COUNTRIES

Ann Weston

Abstract

While the results of the Uruguay Round are generally expected to generate welfare gains, a number of developing countries, in particular some of poorest in Africa, stand to lose, For sub-Saharan Africa losses are estimated at up to 0.5 per cent of GDP. Africa will also lose its privileged status under the Lomé Convention with respect to textiles and clothing, and agriculture. Amongst developing countries, only for East Asia are the results unambiguously positive. Developing countries also will incur costs as a result of the more stringent rules on intellectual property rights and new administrative requirements. The extent to which these may be offset by benefits, such as increased foreign investment, is not known, but the poorer countries will be the least able to share in these benefits. The Final Act includes provisions for compensation in a variety of forms, which now need to be operationalized. Arguments against such compensation have been raised on grounds of setting an undesirable precedent, moral hazard, and negligible need. It has been suggested that African countries themselves could reduce the need for compensation by initiating greater domestic policy changes. These would require complementary adjustment assistance and, thus, a reversal of the recent decline in aid flows, especially to the least developed countries. Low-income food deficit countries will also need additional finance to expand food production in the long term and to cover their increased import bills in the short term. Since the existing funds of the international financial institutions are generally too conditional to qualify as compensation, there is need for a new trade adjustment facility, which should combine assistance for general trade development, food imports and technical support, and be on grant or extremely soft terms.

Introduction

In the year or so following the conclusion of the Uruguay Round there has been considerable effort to review the results of the final package and to gauge their likely impact on various countries, in particular developing countries. One reason was to determine the benefit of these countries' being engaged more actively than before in international trade negotiations. A second was to see whether the concerns raised by particular countries, notably net food importing countries and preference receiving countries, were well-founded. A third was the general interest in international equity - to what extent were developing countries likely to benefit from the offers on market access, the new trade rules and the creation of the World Trade Organisation (WTO)?

This paper sets out to summarize the findings of various studies with respect to the implications for developing countries, both in general and, at a disaggregated level, for the poorest countries, where such information exists. An important question is whether or not some forms of assistance are needed to help countries take full advantage of the new opportunities created by the Round. Also there is interest in countries' capacities to cope with adjustment pressures arising from changes in world markets and to bear the costs of their own commitments in various areas. To make the erosion of special and differential treatment more palatable, a variety of commitments from developed countries were incorporated in the Final Act, ranging from technical and financial assistance to improvements in preferential access to markets of developed countries.

The question now is how to operationalize these commitments.

Part I of the paper reviews the findings with respect to the costs and benefits of the Round for developing countries, disaggregating these wherever possible. Particular attention is given to the issue of lost preferences and increased food import costs, though other important areas are also considered - notably the impact of stricter intellectual property rights as well as the need for administrative and institutional changes.

Part II of the paper deals with the issue of compensation, both the extent and types of compensation offered and alternative measures that seem appropriate for developing countries in general and for the poorest in particular.

I. Costs and benefits

Most studies of the economic effects of the Round conclude that on balance developing countries as a whole stand to gain. Estimates of net welfare gains for them range up to 1.3 per cent of GDP, depending on the number of Uruguay Round provisions incorporated, differences in time-horizon, as well as the counterfactual and model structure. The largest projected gains are in Asia and Latin America - ranging from 0.2 per cent to 3.6 per cent of GDP for South Asia, less than 0.1 per cent to 3.8 per cent of GDP for East Asia, and 0.3 per cent to 1.9 per cent of GDP for Latin America. For sub-Saharan Africa, however, losses of up to 0.5 per cent of GDP are possible, while maximum gains are put at 1.5 per cent of GDP (Hertel et al., 1995, p. 21, and Francois et al., 1995, p. 24 and table 9. The former also shows a possible loss of 0.08 per cent of GDP for Latin America, p. 37).[1]

For developed countries the estimated gains range from a low of 0.05 per cent of GDP in the case of the United States and a high of 6.0 per cent of GDP for EFTA (Francois et al., 1995, table 9; the EFTA estimate reflects large gains from both agricultural and clothing reforms).

Most studies concentrate on tariff cuts, removal of the MFA, and agricultural liberalization, as these are the most easily quantifiable aspects of the Round. Conclusions as to which will have the greatest impact vary somewhat. For instance, in the case of manufactures, one study estimates 81 per cent of the welfare gains (in terms of projected expenditure in 2005 at 1992 prices) would come from tariff cuts, and the rest from expansion of textiles and clothing quotas and the eventual abolition of the MFA (Hertel et al., 1995, table 13, p. 37). Some 35 per cent of the global welfare gains will accrue to developing countries, another 15 per cent to the newly industrialized economies and the rest to the developed countries (ibid., p. 19).

Many studies show, however, that two groups of developing countries stand to lose, at least in the short run. One includes the countries which are beneficiaries of various preferential tariff schemes, notably the Lomé Convention. The second is the net food importing countries. As table 1 shows, both groups include a number of the poorest countries - as many as 33 least developed countries and six low-income countries fall in both categories.

UNCTAD (1995, pp. 10-11) estimates that the least developed countries stand to lose between $300 million and $600 million annually, once the commitments on tariffs and agriculture are fully implemented. This is equal to 3 per cent to 5 per cent of total export earnings; for some countries the losses will be proportionately much higher. In the following, the loss of preferences and the increased prices of food imports will be examined in greater detail.

A.   Loss of preferences

There is a tendency for many studies to be quite dismissive of the benefits of tariff and non-tariff barrier preferences, thereby diminishing the case for compensation. But often these arguments are questionable, as they place too much emphasis on the aggregate and result from too little analysis of individual country or product experience, or possible future changes in production structures. It is ironic that at a time when several countries are undertaking structural reforms to encourage the expansion and diversification of their exports which would help to take better advantage of preferences these will be significantly reduced.

Many authors are extremely sceptical about the impact of losing preferences. For example, Davenport (quoted in DeRosa, 1994, p. 2) estimates that removal of European Union preferences in 1989 would have produced export revenue losses equal to only 0.5 per cent of total African exports. Yeats (cited by Harmsen and Subramanian, p. 34) values OECD preferences for sub-Saharan Africa at $5 billion, giving losses

Table 1

ACP MEMBERS AND FOOD AID RECIPIENTS AMONG THE LEAST DEVELOPED
AND LOW-INCOME COUNTRIES

	ACP member	Food aid recipient		ACP member	Food aid recipient
Least developed countries			Somalia	*	*
			Sudan	*	*
			Tanzania	*	*
Afghanistan		*	Togo	*	*
Burkina Faso	*	*	Tuvalu	*	
Bangladesh		*	Uganda	*	*
Benin	*	*	Vanuatu	*	
Bhutan		*	Yemen		*
Botswana	*	*	Zaire	*	*
Burundi	*	*	Zambia	*	*
Cambodia		*			
Cape Verde	*	*	*Total least developed countries*	*38*	*40*
Central African Republic	*	*			
Chad	*	*			
Comoros	*	*	**Low-income countries**		
Djibouti	*	*			
Equatorial Guinea	*	*	Angola	*	*
Ethiopia		*	Bolivia		*
Guinea-Bissau	*	*	China		*
Gambia	*	*	Cote d'Ivoire	*	
Guinea	*	*	Egypt		*
Haiti		*	Ghana	*	*
Kiribati	*		Guyana	*	
Lao People's Dem. Rep.		*	Honduras		*
Lesotho	*	*	India		*
Liberia	*	*	Indonesia		*
Madagascar	*	*	Kenya	*	*
Malawi	*	*	Nicaragua		*
Maldives		*	Nigeria	*	
Mali	*	*	Pakistan		*
Mauritania	*	*	Philippines		*
Mozambique	*	*	Senegal	*	*
Myanmar		*	Sri Lanka		*
Nepal		*	Tadjikistan		
Niger	*	*	Viet Nam		*
Rwanda	*	*	Zimbabwe	*	*
Samoa	*				
Sao Tome and Principe	*	*	*Total low-income countries*	*8*	*16*
Sierra Leone	*	*			
Solomon Islands	*		**Total**	**46**	**56**

Source: World Food Programme, *1992 Food Aid Review.*

from the Uruguay Round at $900 million or less than 0.3 per cent of 1992 exports. Moreover, it is argued that the full impact of these changes will be felt gradually as the tariff cuts for other suppliers (MFN) will be phased-in over 6 years.

Excluding oil, some $14.6 billion, or 62 per cent of total African exports to the European Union, Japan and the United States are dutiable on a MFN basis (1988 figures, UNDP/UNCTAD, 1994, p. 10). The majority, or $12.7 billion, go to the European Union, of which $12.2 billion receive ACP preferences and $0.2 billion GSP preferences. These preferences will be eroded on average by 30 per cent and 45 per cent respectively. ACP exporters of tropical products will see the largest proportionate preferential loss (51 per cent), followed by exporters of other industrial products (47 per cent), leather and footwear (38 per cent) and non-tropical agriculture (25 per cent). In Japan and the United States, the loss for African exporters on average will be 60 per cent and 40 per cent respectively (ibid.).

These figures treat as equal a cut in a MFN tariff from 40 per cent to 20 per cent and another from 4 per cent to 2 per cent. It may be more meaningful to examine absolute tariff cuts. In the case of the European Union, at least, it appears that heavily protected items will not be given major MFN cuts: "The vast majority of items are subject to tariff cuts of less than 4 percentage points (indeed, in most cases the cut will be 2 percentage points or fewer)" (Stevens and Kennan, 1994, p. 16).

Another problem is that there have been few attempts to evaluate the impact of preference margins on the expansion of exports of individual countries - most analyses are very aggregated, both in terms of products and countries. This is all the more urgent when it is acknowledged that there may be some ACP countries which will be 'seriously affected', and that "the impact on individual countries will need to be closely monitored in the context of Fund- and Bank-supported programmes as the Uruguay Round agreement is implemented" (Harmsen and Subramanian, 1994, p. 34).

Some suggest that the erosion of preferences on non-agricultural exports to the European Union will make 'no real' difference to Africa as over half of its exports are in mining, i.e. coal, crude petroleum, natural gas and other minerals, which are practically duty-free, even for MFN suppliers (Francois et al., 1994, p. 21; as a result, these authors do not bother to include ACP preferential tariffs in their modelling work).

One study identifies major sub-Saharan African exports to the European Union. These were defined as products from any one country which exceeded ECU 10 million in 1992 or products exported by more than 10 countries and which exceeded ECU 1 million (Stevens and Kennan 1994, p. 37). Excluding items which faced a tariff cut of less than 5 percentage points produced a shorter list of only 39 products (at the 8-digit level) or some 5.2 per cent of sub-Saharan African exports, worth ECU 1.3 billion in 1992. For these the loss (which is calculated as the amount by which ACP exporters would have to cut their prices to maintain the same price margin with respect to other developing country exporters) is put at around ECU 50 million, i.e. 4.1 per cent of the shortlist or 0.2 per cent of sub-Saharan African exports overall, of which half will be in coffee. While the price adjustments required of ACP exporters would be small, especially compared to recent changes in world market prices for some of their exports, it should be feasible to find compensating improvements to the Lomé Convention.

The changes in tariffs on temperate and tropical agricultural, and industrial products are likely to put the least developed countries at a disadvantage, in particular ACP and African countries. Their net export losses are estimated at 1.9 per cent and 1.5 per cent respectively (Page and Davenport, 1994, p. 62). Almost all individual sub-Saharan African countries would lose this way, notably Ethiopia (5.9 per cent), Malawi (5.3 per cent) and Mozambique (4.6 per cent). Another study suggests that Swaziland would be the most affected as its exports to the European Union have the highest average preferential margin of any sub-Saharan African country, at 5.4 per cent points (Harrold, 1995, p. 12). However, focus should be the tariff margin on dutiable products, not all exports.

In the case of the GSP, margins will fall by only 18 per cent on average - 23 per cent in the European Union, 9 per cent in the United States and 15 per cent in Japan - compared to the 40 per cent MFN cut (because of differences in product composition of MFN and GSP trade). Moreover, according to UNCTAD in absolute terms this would amount to a small reduction in tariff margins as the MFN tariffs on most GSP-covered items are small (Harmsen and Subramanian, 1994, p. 29). The GSP margin for least developed countries will be cut by 3 percentage points in the European Union and Japan, and 2 percentage points in the United States (UNCTAD, 1995, p. 7). Static losses resulting from the erosion of GSP are estimated at some ECU 44 million or 3.4 per cent of the value of all developing countries' major industrial exports to the European Union (Stevens and Kennan,

1994, p. 18). For least developed countries, lower preferences are expected to cut exports by between $163 million and $265 million (UNCTAD, 1995, p.10).

Where MFN tariffs continue to be significant for a number of products in various markets (notably agricultural products, clothing and various end-products), it may be possible to compensate countries by maintaining, binding or enlarging preferential margins or extending them to new products. This is particularly the case for temperate agricultural products, where the tariffication of various import restrictions, and the use of tariff quotas, should make it possible to maintain preferences (on this, more below). Already the European Union is planning to make cuts in its GSP rates in partial compensation. This would increase the losses to the ACP, however.

While much of the debate on preferences has focused on tariffs, another important area is that of non-tariff barriers (NTBs). Indeed, one study concludes that "most of the potential benefits of trade liberalization under the guise of the Round hinge on NTB elimination instead of tariffs" (Francois et al., 1995, p. 26). Africa would lose across-the-board on manufactures - as much as 0.5 per cent of GDP in 2005 or $1.23 billion at 1992 prices - of which half is due to the end of clothing restraints under the MFA and half to tariff cuts (Hertel et al., 1995, p.37).

Africa will not enjoy the same gains from the ending of the MFA as expected by most other developing country exporters, notably in Asia and, to a lesser extent, Latin America. "(U)nder all specifications, African production of clothing shrinks ... . At the same time, production of textiles in Africa expands under all model specifications ... . The difference in impact between textiles and clothing likely reflects relative preference erosion. Clothing producers competing with Africa initially face much more stringent protection than competing textile producers do ..." (Francois, et al., 1994, p. 21). The abolition of the MFA removes the strong growth possibilities in clothing for sub-Saharan Africa; in the absence of any change in the MFA, apparel output in Africa would rise by 111 per cent over a ten-year period, whereas with the Round it will only grow by 30 per cent (Hertel et al., 1995, pp. 22-23).

Most of the gains in the Uruguay Round to other developing countries come from the liberalization of trade in textiles and clothing. For example, it will lead to a 4.5 per cent increase in exports from South Asia (from their 1992 level) and a 6.1 per cent increase for exports from other Asian countries. But for the

ACP and the least developed countries, it will produce losses equal to 0.2 per cent of their exports in 1992 (Page and Davenport, 1994, p. 62). Countries particularly affected include Bangladesh (18.9 per cent decline in exports), Mauritius (-16.5 per cent) and Jamaica (-7.6 per cent).

Other analysts, however, are more sceptical about the prospects for liberalization of the developed countries' textile and clothing markets, and thus tend to downplay the potential negative impact on more preferred suppliers. "The best conclusion that can be reached at this stage ... is that the Uruguay Round will not result in any substantial improvement in developing country access to the European market in the short term. Perhaps by the end of this century and the beginning of the next there may start to be important openings. But they are not yet in evidence." (Stevens and Kennan, 1994, p. 21).

In the area of agriculture, it is unclear whether ACP suppliers will continue to enjoy preferred access for their beef, sugar and other exports. Some have argued that the new agricultural import rules (see below) will allow the ACP to maintain current levels of access and preference (Harmsen and Subramanian, 1994, p. 34; Harrold, 1995, p. 15; Page and Davenport, 1994, p. 27). As these account for two-thirds of preferences for sub-Saharan Africa, not taking this possibility into account will overstate their likely losses. Import restrictions might be converted into tariff quotas, allowing allocations to the same exporting countries as under the former regime (Ingco 1995, p. 47). It is important to determine whether this is in fact the case, or whether this is really an issue still to be resolved in the renegotiations of the Lomé Convention. The opposition to the new European Union tariff quota arrangement for bananas, although not fully analogous, suggests no one should assume that the Lomé preferences for other agricultural products will be maintained.

In fact, there may only be limited openings in the European Union market for sensitive agricultural products before the end of the century, thus diminishing concerns about erosion of preferences. Besides the possibility of special safeguard controls if imports surge, only small tariff cuts are proposed - of some 5.8 percentage points on average from very high tariff levels (Stevens and Kennan, 1994, p. 26).

Many would argue that preferential trade is not a reliable long-term strategy, even for the poorest countries. Some consider ACP preferences a market distortion, to the extent that they are only allowed by the GATT/WTO through a waiver (in contrast to preferences under regional trade agreements), while the GSP is not even binding. Experience with the GSP has shown that preferences are becoming increasingly conditional. They may have distracted beneficiary countries from the adoption of alternative and more effective export promotion policies and from diversifying both products and markets. One view is that preferences under the Lomé Convention have contributed to sub-Saharan Africa's very heavy dependence on the European Union market, which accounts for 51 per cent of their exports (Harrold, 1995, p. 8). However, while the rents from sugar and banana exports may have discouraged diversification in the Caribbean, there is less evidence of this being the case for sugar or beef exporting countries in Africa, like Zimbabwe or Kenya (Stevens and Kennan, 1994, p. 30). Rather, the loss of preferences may well hinder the process of product diversification, something that is already beginning.

Finally, several studies point to the potential export gains for Africa as a result of increased world demand, expanded and more certain market access from binding MFN reductions - and an increase in the share of trade which is duty-free - although there would still be problems of tariff escalation (e.g. Harrold, 1995). "(T)he group of exporters that will benefit from high proportionate cuts in tariffs on metals, nonelectric machinery, wood, pulp, paper, and furniture includes Cameroon, Ghana, ... although ... the initial level of tariffs is already quite low for most of these products ... . The group of countries that on the basis of its export structure is less well positioned to benefit from widened market access, includes, for example, Ecuador, Honduras and Kenya. The export earnings of these countries are heavily dependent on industrial products where absolute tariff cuts are limited, such as leather, rubber, footwear, travel goods, fish and fish products" (Harmsen and Subramanian, 1994, p. 9).

While African countries may be able to offset losses in the European Union market by increased opportunities elsewhere, this will be a long-term phenomenon. The geographic concentration of African exports has resulted not only from preferential access, but also from other factors such as poor transport links, inadequate market information, and other structural constraints, some of them dating from the colonial period. These will need to be overcome before exports to non-European markets increase. It has also been suggested that supply constraints could be reduced by countries liberalizing their own trade policies (Harrold, 1995).

To conclude, the erosion of preferences will impose small, but real, costs on countries that can least afford them, notably the least developed and low-income countries. The Round may produce new opportunities elsewhere for these countries, which in the long term offset their preferential losses, but in the meantime ways must be found to compensate them, either through expanding and binding preferences, or financially. These issues are taken up further below.

B. Increased food import prices

There is also some scepticism about the effects of the Uruguay Round on food import costs and the need for compensation. This is largely because the final agreement on agricultural policy changes was much less extensive than expected, mitigating upward pressures on world prices and the availability of surpluses for food aid. Another reason is that several developed countries were already liberalizing their agricultural policies, and some of the observed changes in world prices will reflect these changes rather than being due to the Round itself. It is argued that compensation should only be given for the latter (Page and Davenport, 1994, p. 34). Moreover, several analysts suggest that the emphasis should be on the net effect of the Round, i.e. including a possible increase in agricultural export earnings because of higher world prices and/or more open markets, as well as increases in domestic agricultural production.

The new agricultural rules are estimated to produce welfare losses for Africa ranging from 0.10 per cent to 0.30 per cent of 1992 GDP (though in one scenario a 0.23 per cent gain in GDP is projected, Francois et al., 1995, table 17), and for South Asia from 0.05 per cent to 0.10 per cent of GDP. For Latin America, the range is -0.01 per cent to +0.70 per cent of GDP. Only for East Asia are the gains unambiguously positive, up to 1.10 per cent of GDP. For the developed countries, the changes range from a loss of 0.11 per cent to a gain of 1.20 per cent of GDP - with both extremes being for EFTA (Francois et al., 1995).

Another set of provisional estimates for Africa's net income losses, based on an ex-post evaluation of the tariffication process, ranges from $1.3 billion to $2.5 billion by the year 2002 (in 1992 dollars). This concentrates primarily on the short-term impact of tariffication in agriculture but also includes some measure of the changes in manufacturing. Losses as a share of GDP are equal to 0.1 per cent for Nigeria, between 0.2 and 0.4 per cent for South Africa, and between 0.2 and 0.3 per cent for other African countries (Goldin and van der Mensbrugghe, 1995, p. 29). This is a one-half to three-quarters of earlier estimates of between $3.1 billion and $3.3 billion (ibid.). The OECD, by contrast, is expected to gain from between $14 billion and $178.6 billion, while global gains range from $25.4 billion to $235 billion. The range reflects different assumptions about the base period against which to assess liberalization and the inclusion of cuts in input subsidies. The study focuses on tariffication and changes in tariffs, rather than other reforms. It concludes: "The overall gains estimated by the model should not mask the losses, particularly as these are concentrated in vulnerable least developed countries. For these countries, vigilance and the guarantee of the support of the international community is required so that the overwhelming gains of the Uruguay Round are not tarnished by the unacceptable suffering of those unfortunate enough to suffer the marginal negative consequences" (p. 23). On the other hand, it also notes that the price effects of the Round will be less than those resulting from normal instability in world markets, that phasing-in will be slow (taking 5-10 years), and that food importing countries may improve their welfare through unilateral liberalization.

The limits on liberalization in the Round are the result of the limited reductions in border protection, export subsidies and domestic support measures. Most of the reforms have focused on domestic support mechanisms (Ingco, 1995, p. 27). The conversion of non-tariff to tariff measures could lead to more significant cuts in the future: "the long-run implications can hardly be overstated". But for now, 'dirty tariffication' (i.e. binding tariffs well above existing levels), combined with low tariff reductions and the possibility of variable tariffs set between existing and bound rates (Ingco 1995, p. 29), has limited liberalization. This means less diversion of trade from countries/products receiving preferences, and fewer expanded export opportunities where this is not the case. "Tariffication will not likely have a significant effect on trade flows and prices in the next several years. ... (W)hile the Round achieved new transparency in import protection, this came at the expense of significant liberalization in most products" (Ingco, 1995, p. 51).

To illustrate, for all developed countries the differential between the average new tariff and the tariff equivalent of past protection is 200 per cent for rice, and 63 per cent for sugar (Ingco, 1995, p. 23). Tariff reductions are very uneven across products. The target 36 per cent is expressed in terms of an unweighted average; many countries have made larger cuts for non-sensitive, low-tariff items than for sensitive items (e.g. sugar in the European Union) - though there is a minimum target of 15 per cent for all products. Even after the 15 per cent cut, the tariff equivalents of many commodities will remain above the level of protection from 1982 to 1993 (p. 27). This is especially the case in the developed countries (except Japan). In the European Union, the only sector with protection reduced somewhat from the long-term average is beef, and then only from 97 per cent to 83 per cent (Ingco, 1995, p. 43) .

Many developing countries have bound their tariffs well above existing levels, but to a lesser extent than developed countries. In general, the allowable levels of protection for developing countries are well below past levels in developed countries. The highest level of uniform ceiling bindings in sub-Saharan Africa are those of Nigeria (230 per cent), Kenya (100 per cent), and Senegal (180 per cent) (Ingco, 1995, p. 37). They are also quite high in the poorer Asian countries (e.g. Bangladesh 200 per cent) (ibid., p. 35).

The limited liberalization finally achieved in the Round limits the likelihood of major food price increases. For example, "it is difficult to envision that the long-term increase in the aggregate price of farm products will be more than about 1-2 percent" (DeRosa, 1994, p. 8). This compares with earlier projections of increases of as much as 18.3 per cent (rice) and 7.5 per cent (wheat) (ibid., p. 8a); and 4 to 10 per cent in the medium term for these products (Harmsen and Subramanian, 1994, p. 14). The GATT estimates an average 5 per cent price rise (Page and Davenport, 1994, p. 33). The world price of rice may rise by 0.9 per cent, sugar by 5.2 per cent, wheat by 3.6 per cent and coarse grains by 1.9 per cent after all the lags have worked out (ibid.). This is over and above the predicted change in world prices in the absence of the Round of 12.7 per cent for rice, -8.9 per cent for wheat, and -27.3 per cent for coarse grains (ibid.). Another set of estimates, however, suggest that price increases as a result of the Round would be more substantial - ranging from 4 per cent in the case of maize to 7 per cent for wheat and 8 per cent for rice - on top of predicted price changes without the Round of +3 per cent , -3 per cent and +7 per cent respectively.[2]

There is little consensus on the effects of the Uruguay Round on trade in temperate agricultural goods (Page and Davenport 1994, p. 31). Estimated effects vary according to the region/country and product in question, the structure of the underlying model and, for the estimates that were made before the Round was concluded, assumptions about what it would achieve (p. 34). For instance, many estimates do not account for possible supply responses of non-subsidized producers which could mitigate the price increases (Harmsen and Subramanian, 1994, p. 14). Others do not allow for the possible substitution of coarse grains for wheat and rice (Harrold, 1995).

A particular issue is the impact on sub-Saharan Africa's capacity to import food. Net food imports in 1989 amounted to $10.4 billion for Africa as a whole and $2.7 billion for sub-Saharan Africa, with gross imports of $14 billion and $5 billion respectively (UNDP/UNCTAD, 1994, p. 8). Cuts of 20 per cent in domestic support and 21 per cent in export subsidies would lead to increased import costs of $808 million and net income losses of $1.1 billion for Africa (p. 11). The FAO estimates that Africa's food import bill is likely to grow from an average of $6.0 billion in 1987-1989 to $10.5 billion in the year 2000, of which $0.5 billion, or 11 per cent of the increase, will be due to the effect of the Uruguay Round. For the low-income food-deficit countries (LIFD) in Africa the cost of the Uruguay Round will be $0.2 billion or 7 per cent of the projected $2.8 billion increase in food import costs (FAO, 1995, table 5; LIFD countries in the Far East, including South Asia, would experience the greatest costs - of some $1 billion or 19 per cent of the increase in their food import bill). Finally, UNCTAD (1995, p.10) estimates that the food import bill of the least developed countries will increase by 5 per cent to 10 per cent, i.e. $146 million to $292 million. Another source, however, states that sub-Saharan Africa as a whole has a positive trade balance in food, with only 15 countries having a deficit - notably Angola, Congo, Gabon, Liberia, Nigeria, Togo and Zambia - of $2 billion annually or 3 per cent of their total import bill (Harrold 1995, p. 18). If prices rise by 5 per cent, this will lead to a 0.15 per cent increase in their total import bill.

The FAO (1995, table 5) estimates that Africa's agricultural trade balance will deteriorate by as much as $1.5 billion, shifting from a surplus of $1 billion to a deficit of $0.5 billion. Agricultural trade is particularly important to the 21 low-income, non-fuel exporting, countries in sub-Saharan Africa, accounting for 44 per cent of exports and 19 per cent of imports, whereas for non-fuel exporting sub-Saharan Africa as a whole the shares are 20 per cent and 13 per cent respectively (DeRosa, 1994, pp. 9-10). Food imports are especially critical for the low-income countries, all of which are also food-deficit countries, and account for 76 per cent of agricultural imports, of which cereals are 52 per cent. According

to some estimates, the Round will have a net positive effect on sub-Saharan Africa's agricultural trade balance as exports expand more than imports (DeRosa, 1994, p. 11). But this is more likely to be the case for middle-income countries than for low-income countries. Only 6 of the 21 food-deficit countries will see trade gains, and for the 21 countries taken together the estimated losses ($95 million) are double the gains ($46 million). Some 56 per cent of increased import costs are for cereals. For 23 sub-Saharan African countries altogether the losses will outweigh the gains. The increased import costs as a share of total imports range from 3.2 per cent for Mauritania to 0.1 per cent for Uganda with an overall average of 0.4 per cent (see table 2).

As these trade imbalances are likely to be unsustainable, countries may have to adjust their exchange rates. Besides devaluation, food-deficit low-income countries may have to lower the volume of their food imports, decreasing domestic food availability. The FAO (1995, table 6) forecasts that the Uruguay Round will result in LIFD countries slightly lowering their per capita food consumption, to just below the level recorded in 1987-1989. If imports are cut, all but four low-income countries will be able to finance their higher cereal costs through higher export earnings (DeRosa, 1994). But agricultural exports from the ACP countries to the European Union, which previously enjoyed preferences linked to internal European Union prices, will experience lower prices as the European Union protection is cut. One study assumes that the preferential margin of about 50 per cent will be maintained (though, as explained above, this remains uncertain) thus preventing any shift to third country producers. On this basis, ACP beef prices may fall by 18 per cent as both levies and the internal price of the European Union are reduced. For sugar, an 11 per cent price cut will only marginally be compensated by the 5 per cent rise in the world sugar price. Rice prices of ACP countries are expected to fall by 9.5 per cent - the result of internal European Union prices falling by 19 per cent and the ACP price being half-way between world and European Union prices (Page and Davenport, 1994, pp. 26-27).

The importance of domestic reforms has also been stressed as a means for African countries to "substantially reduce the possible adverse consequences of the Uruguay Round agreement, and even achieve net economic gains ... (T)he initial negative effects to net importers of food and other farm goods of the international price increases may be turned into positive long-term effects in cases with

Table 2

TRADE IN AGRICULTURE OF SUB-SAHARAN AFRICAN COUNTRIES

($million)

	Increase in import bill (A)	Total imports (B)	Total exports (C)	A/B (Per cent)	A/C (Per cent)	Memo item: Increase in export revenue
All countries	*206.5*	*47005*	*44466*	*0.4*	*0.5*	*307.8*
Low-income countries	*94.6*	*11472*	*6441*	*0.8*	*1.5*	*46.5*
Benin	4.1	640	275	0.6	1.5	5.2
Burkina Faso	4.5	580	326	0.8	1.4	5.1
Burundi	1.2	238	80	0.5	1.5	0.2
Central African Republic	1.3	148	136	0.9	1.0	0.6
Chad	1.2	407	201	0.3	0.6	3.7
Comoros	0.9	59	21	1.5	4.3	0.0
Equatorial Guinea	0.5	63	36	0.8	1.4	0.0
Ethiopia	10.9	661	239	1.6	4.6	1.8
Gambia	3.4	206	48	1.7	7.1	0.5
Ghana	10.0	1343	972	0.7	1.0	1.1
Guinea	6.2	713	699	0.9	0.9	0.3
Guinea-Bissau	1.2	83	15	1.4	8.0	0.0
Kenya	9.2	1948	1173	0.5	0.8	5.0
Lesotho	4.3	646	65	0.7	6.6	0.9
Madagascar	2.7	495	323	0.5	0.8	3.7
Malawi	3.7	688	430	0.5	0.9	7.5
Mali	5.8	656	359	0.9	1.6	8.3
Mauritania	6.9	218	443	3.2	1.6	0.0
Mozambique	10.0	887	155	1.1	6.5	2.2
Niger	4.4	499	353	0.9	1.2	0.2
Rwanda	2.0	294	90	0.7	2.2	0.2
Middle-income countries	*111.9*	*35533*	*38024*	*0.3*	*0.3*	*261.3*
Botswana	4.2	2313	2204	0.2	0.2	5.0
Cape Verde	1.5	137	9	1.1	16.7	0.0
Cote d'Ivoire	12.5	2085	2932	0.6	0.4	16.2
Djibouti	2.4	218	21	1.1	11.4	0.0
Liberia	2.8	123	200	2.3	1.4	0.0
Mauritius	6.0	1601	1220	0.4	0.5	66.2
Namibia	2.9	1287	1178	0.2	0.2	2.6
Sao Tome and Principe	0.2	31	14	0.6	1.4	0.0
Senegal	12.8	1343	720	1.0	1.8	8.6
Seychelles	0.9	183	49	0.5	1.8	0.0
Sierra Leone	3.0	156	146	1.9	2.1	0.0
Somalia	3.6	367	82	1.0	4.4	0.0
South Africa	26.3	17532	23661	0.2	0.1	79.2
Sudan	8.4	921	480	0.9	1.8	15.3
Swaziland	2.6	721	567	0.4	0.5	31.0
Tanzania	3.3	1477	296	0.2	1.1	6.5
Togo	2.7	608	279	0.4	1.0	4.2
Uganda	0.8	535	167	0.1	0.5	1.6
Zaire	6.3	765	876	0.8	0.7	0.6
Zambia	2.3	991	1209	0.2	0.2	2.0
Zimbabwe	6.3	2139	1614	0.3	0.4	22.2

Source: DeRosa (1994) Tables 4 and 5.

Note: Figures for total imports and exports are the annual average in 1990-92.

a high degree of price transmission to domestic farmers and where non-price constraints to production are not seriously binding" (DeRosa, 1994, p. 13).

The limited agricultural liberalization resulting from the Uruguay Round, will nonetheless result in higher food prices and losses for food-deficit countries, many of which are among the poorest countries. While in the longer term they may be able to offset some of these losses by expanding domestic production as well as agricultural and other exports, in the shorter term they face the prospect of increased hardship.

C.   Other costs

There are several other areas where the possibility of costs or losses for developing countries as a result of the Round has been raised, though in most cases they tend to be overlooked, partly because they are difficult to quantify. Examples include: the increased cost of technology, seeds and pharmaceuticals as a result of increased intellectual property protection; and the bureaucratic or human resource costs of creating and managing the new trade laws and institutions.

In the case of intellectual property rights (IPRs), many developing countries will have to extend protection both horizontally, introducing IPRs for the first time in several new areas, and vertically, raising protection levels in others. For instance as many as 25 countries do not provide patents for pharmaceutical products, and 13 for chemical products, while 57 do not protect computer software (Primo Braga, 1994, p. 32). From a static perspective, the new rules will lead to a transfer in rent primarily from the developing to the developed countries. Estimates of annual static welfare losses range from $67 million to $387 million for Argentina, $220 million to $1.3 billion for India, $153 million to $879 million for Brazil, and $75 million to $428 million for Mexico (Harmsen and Subramanian, 1994, p. 25). In addition, there will be considerable bureaucratic costs: "Issues like proper enforcement and compulsory licensing practices, for example, will demand numerous additional changes in national legislation and procedures, particularly in developing countries. It will be a challenge for the over-extended judicial systems of most developing countries to ensure effective and appropriate means of enforcement..." (Primo Braga, p. 33).

It is possible that stronger IPRs will help to attract foreign direct investment and the transfer of technology to developing countries while they may

benefit from increased export earnings (Primo Braga 1995, p. 50). Also, the costs will be diluted if the long transitional periods allowed by the Final Act are followed. In the case of the least developed countries these may be extended beyond 11 years. But there is pressure on countries to accelerate implementation of stronger IPRs, e.g. in order to qualify for additional preferences under the European Union's GSP, and to be considered eligible for NAFTA membership.

Another area is the cost of trade liberalization. While the prevailing view is that domestic liberalization will bring welfare gains, some analysts acknowledge that "there is no one magic level of protection to target ... " and given the inevitable dislocations, "the transition has to be managed in an orderly manner". Also, given that trade policies often serve non-trade objectives (notably fiscal, but also balance of payments), "alternative policy instruments must be instituted" (Calika and Corsepius, 1994, pp. 62-63). For instance, fiscal reform is needed as trade taxes still account for a substantial share of total tax revenue in some countries. There is also a need for complementary measures such as social safety nets, and technical assistance to increase administrative capacities. It is generally accepted that low-income countries should be granted financial assistance during the period of trade reform to help sustain their liberalization. Therefore, World Bank and IMF funds have been associated with various trade reform measures.

II.   Compensation

A number of different arguments have been made about compensation. Low estimates of losses have been used to dismiss calls for compensation in the form of financial assistance or expanded preferences, even though these were explicitly provided for in the Final Act. Where losses occur, it is argued, developing countries should offset them by undertaking further domestic liberalization. Other problems are moral hazard and precedent-setting (see below). There is broad support, however, for technical assistance. These points are examined before turning to the issue of what modalities might be considered for compensation.

At one extreme is the view that "the best advice to sub-Saharan African countries in this regard is to forget about the compensation issue, and get on with the reforms that count. ... It is noted that the Uruguay Round document raises the possibility of financial assistance for the least developed countries from the international organizations: in this author's view that would not be a good use of scarce international development resources. It may well be that sub-Saharan African countries need and deserve to receive technical assistance to help them comply with the Uruguay Round, and this is envisaged in the agreement, but that is quite different from the compensation issue" (Harrold, 1994, p. 53).

There is a broader agreement, though still not unanimous, that countries could offset some of their own losses by undertaking domestic liberalization, and even that countries in sub-Saharan Africa would experience net gains from the Uruguay Round if they had undertaken greater domestic liberalization, by removing quantity restrictions and reducing tariffs. For example, it is noted that 15 sub-Saharan African countries (accounting for more than 50 per cent of sub-Saharan Africa's GDP) still have an average nominal tariff of 37.6 per cent (Harrold, 1995, p. 55). Import prices of manufactures in sub-Saharan Africa will fall by only 0.1 per cent, which means that their Uruguay Round commitments will impose very little discipline on domestic protection (Hertel et al., 1995, p. 26). "The losses from the global tariff reduction package are a consequence of deteriorations in the terms of trade not offset by sizeable efficiency gains from liberalization of the region's own trade policies. In other regions, where more substantial liberalization is undertaken, these efficiency gains have been sufficient to outweigh any terms-of-trade losses. Further liberalization seems the most promising approach to overcome the adverse consequences of the current outcome" (Hertel et al., 1995, p. 21). Yet this would require complementary structural reforms, with external financial support as well as technical assistance, for the reasons mentioned above, and take some time to materialize.

Some authors question whether compensation is appropriate for the removal of distortions (such as tariff preferences), especially as it may create a precedent which complicates future negotiations, as well as a moral hazard. "Compensating the costs of losing the benefits of past distortions is less defensible. If this principle is accepted as a new trading rule, negotiating any reduction in trade barriers in future will be complicated by adding a third party, with an interest in preventing reform, to the traditional GATT model of negotiations between principal importers and exporters" (Page and Davenport, 1994, p. 65). In addition, the Final Act is argued to be unfair in that it provides for compensation for one type of loss, namely subsidized food imports, but neither for loss of tariff

preferences nor the MFA, even though the latter is projected to cause greater losses for a number of countries (ibid.). But there are several other references to assistance in the treaty, ranging from the extension of preferences to technical assistance in a variety of areas, which, presumably, should be considered forms of compensation, even if very partial.

Other questions are whether the right to compensation should be automatic (as usual in other parts of the GATT once a claim is found to be justified) or conditional on the affected countries making changes in their economic or other policies (Page and Davenport, 1994, p. 34), and whether it should be dependent on net losses, given that these are not explicitly mentioned in the Final Act.

There are several modalities for ensuring adequate compensation for developing countries affected by the Round. Here the need for increased aid, including technical assistance, and expanded preferences are considered in turn. The new WTO has an important role to play, both in monitoring the impact of the new international trade regime on the poorest countries, and in the delivery of technical assistance. This would complement work by UNCTAD and the International Trade Centre (ITC). Finally, the issue of support from the international financial institutions is considered.

A. Increased aid

As already discussed, a number of the poorest countries need assistance in three areas: first, to cover the increased costs of imports, notably food, technology and other intellectual property; second, to adjust to import liberalization, the new trade rules, and new export opportunities; and third, to cover cuts in export preferences. Even though developed countries are generally forecast to experience large gains as a result of the Round, there is no legal obligation in the Final Act for them to compensate the poorest countries for their losses in each of these three areas. Instead, there is a series of piecemeal and, for the most part, vague commitments to assistance (Weston, 1994). For instance, there will be technical cooperation on the drafting and enforcement of intellectual property laws, the establishment of standardizing bodies, and improvements in sanitary and phytosanitary standards, while no help has been agreed in the area of trade remedy legislation. In some cases this assistance will be in the form of advice, credits, donations, or grants, in others on mutually agreed terms. The potentially higher costs of technology are to be offset by developed country government 'incentives' to their private sectors to transfer technology to the least developed countries.

The commitments are clearer in the case of the least developed and net food importing countries. Least developed countries "shall be accorded substantially increased technical assistance in the development, strengthening and diversification of their production and export bases ... to enable them to maximize the benefits from liberalized access to markets" (Decision on Measures in favour of Least Developed Countries). For net food importing countries, an increasing proportion of food aid is to be in grant form or on appropriate concessional terms and assistance will be given to improving agricultural productivity and infrastructure. In addition, existing or new financing facilities in the IFIs are expected to cover short-term financing needs. Meeting these various commitments will require additional resources - and, thus, a reversal of the recent trend: since 1992 aid from OECD countries and multilateral organizations to least developed countries has fallen by 7.9 per cent (OECD, 1994, p. 76).

The OECD Development Assistance Committee should play a role, in conjunction with the WTO, in monitoring, encouraging and coordinating donor country follow-up to the Round. At least two countries (Canada and Switzerland) have commissioned studies to determine the impact of the Round on selected aid recipients (Weston, 1994 and Degbelo et al., 1994). Such initiatives should be coordinated to avoid duplication.

On the issue of food, the Committee on Food Aid under the Food Aid Convention is expected to review poorer countries' needs for additional food aid and to ensure an increasing proportion is fully in grant form or other concessional terms. The World Food Programme should analyze the possible reduced availability of food aid and likely change in food import costs following the Uruguay Round.

The FAO (1995) has recommended at least two ways to increase assistance to LIFD countries. One is a new financing facility for food production. This would promote public and private sector investments in the production of crops and in countries where the Round has created new economic opportunities. The second is a short-term financing facility to cover increased import costs. Finance would be triggered by a rise in a world food price index above a certain threshold, without any attempt to determine the exact

impact of the Round. The amounts available would be linked to the price change and the volume of a country's imports in a base year or as necessary to prevent any decline in its per capita consumption. They would be on grant terms, as aid-in-kind or tied cash aid, and additional to existing flows. The facility would be available for the ten years over which the Round's agricultural commitments will be phased in (though the possibility of further agricultural liberalization being negotiated in the WTO suggests that such a facility might need to be extended beyond ten years).

B.   *Expansion of preferences*

Erosion of preferences could be offset in various ways. For ACP industrial products, less stringent rules of origin, especially for textiles and clothing, could help to offset some of the losses arising from MFN tariff cuts, proposed extensions to the European Union's GSP, and the ending of the MFA. For some agricultural products, it should be possible to maintain or even increase preferential margins, especially for products previously facing quotas or variable levies which have now been tariffied (e.g. beef, sugar, rice and bananas). In other developed countries, GSP schemes should be reviewed and expanded with a view to improving the coverage of exports from least developed and low-income countries, their usage of preferences and the depth of tariff cuts. Supervision of these changes should be a joint responsibility of the UNCTAD Special Committee on Preferences and the WTO Committee on Trade and Development (see below). There should be an agreement in the WTO that such preferences will not be challenged (as they could be under the new provisions for reviewing waivers) on the grounds that they are part of the commitment to offset the least developed countries' losses. Making GSP schemes binding for the least developed, and even for low-income countries, should also be considered.

C.   *The WTO and other agencies*

The WTO has several bodies which should be required both to monitor the costs and also to help design and monitor implementation of compensatory action. The extent to which the WTO will be able to deliver some of this compensation itself is less clear. A distinction needs to be made between the WTO as a body overseeing the implementation of the Uruguay Round and the WTO Secretariat. Several WTO committees, notably the Committee on Trade and

Development (CTD), the Committee on Agriculture and the General Council, all have an important role to play in ensuring that the interests of the least developed countries are monitored and the offers of assistance honoured. The Secretariat will be crucial in monitoring and evaluating the impact of the Round and subsequent changes in international trade policy affecting these countries, as well as in delivering, and organizing others to provide, technical assistance.

The CTD has been given the responsibility of periodically reviewing the special provisions in the Multilateral Trade Agreements in favour of developing and least developed country members and reporting to the General Council for appropriate action (Agreement establishing the WTO, 1994, Article IV.7). The CTD will act as a focal point for the WTO's development work and to coordinate with other multilateral agencies. It is also to consider measures to assist developing countries in the expansion of trade and investment opportunities, and to support their own trade liberalization (terms of reference elaborated at the end of January 1995 (WT/L/46)). Finally, it will produce guidelines and monitor the WTO's technical cooperation activities for developing countries. If other elements of its work become overwhelming, it might be useful to delegate work relating to least developed countries to a separate sub-Committee, based on the former GATT sub-Committee on Trade of Least Developed Countries.

The WTO Committee on Agriculture will monitor the situation of least developed and net food importing countries. Similarly, other bodies will be responsible for reviewing the operations and specific commitments to developing countries under their agreement. For example, the Textiles Monitoring Body, under the Council for Trade in Goods, will oversee implementation of the textiles and clothing agreement; the Council for Trade-Related Aspects of Intellectual Property Rights (TRIPs) will monitor whether developed countries provide technical and financial cooperation for the least developed and other developing countries to strengthen their enforcement of intellectual property rights.

Finally, the General Council will oversee the Trade Policy Review Body in charge of the Trade Policy Review Mechanism. The country-specific reviews, which it undertakes, could be used to evaluate the extent to which developed countries are meeting their Uruguay Round commitments and especially those most relevant to developing countries. The costs of failure to do so could be estimated and appropriate compensation suggested. Similarly, the issue of compensatory action including technical assistance could be dealt with in the reviews of developing countries' trade policies and performance.

The WTO Secretariat will service some of these committees. Both the creation of a Development Division and the strengthening of the Technical Cooperation and Training Division are "expected to raise substantially the ability of GATT to respond to the needs of developing members" (GATT, 1994a, p. 8). Within the Development Division, a Special Unit for Least Developed countries will serve as a focal point for issues relating to these countries though issues may then be passed on to other relevant divisions.

The resources available to the WTO have been expanded modestly, by about 10 per cent above GATT levels (roughly an additional 18 professionals on a previous total of some 150 operational professionals), but member countries may agree to further increases in subsequent years. The Development Division will have four professionals and Technical Cooperation seven (compared to five in the past). In 1995 some SFr 644,000 will be available for technical cooperation missions out of a total WTO budget of SFr 105 million, with a further SFr 1.2 million for trade policy training courses, and WTO will continue the GATT's joint funding with UNCTAD of the ITC, providing some SFr 13.4 million.

These changes appear inadequate for the WTO to satisfy developing countries' increasing needs for technical assistance, let alone to cover the costs of strengthening their trade-investment infrastructure. While the WTO's responsibility for the latter may be debatable, there appears to be consensus that it has a major responsibility for training developing country officials.[3] Additional funding may be available on an ad hoc basis through trust funds, i.e. financed by individual donors and normally earmarked for a specific purpose (e.g., in the past a Swiss fund was used to train East European trade officials). Considerably more resources could be made available to the WTO through the creation of a global trust fund, allowing it to expand its professional staff and/or to draw on a pool of international experts as needed by developing country members.

Another possibility is for donor Governments to provide technical assistance directly. For example, if a developing country requests the Committee on Anti-Dumping Practices to help with the creation of new anti-dumping mechanisms, another country would volunteer to send someone from its customs agency, perhaps accompanying a WTO officer.

Alternatively, the WTO could turn to another international organization to do this. Other agencies have some funds and mechanisms for training, for example, WIPO in the area of intellectual property rights, the WHO in the area of sanitary standards, and UNCTAD in services. This complementarity will be assisted by the fact that many specialized agencies have observer status at the WTO. For example, the WIPO is an observer at the Committee on TRIPs meetings and so could respond to requests for help with implementing new legislation in this area. Another possibility would be the use of UNDP resources (though this might be complicated by the WTO's reluctance to operate as a United Nations executing agency).

There is a need for close collaboration between the WTO and UNCTAD. UNCTAD has considerable experience in analyzing the implications of trends in international trade on developing countries (see, for example, UNCTAD, 1994), providing a wide range of technical assistance, and coordinating the work of other agencies in this area, as well as having specific responsibilities for the least developed countries. Again, the issue of resource allocation needs to be addressed if UNCTAD is to expand its work in this area.

The ITC could also be critical in the follow-up to the Round. It plans to build on earlier operational activities to facilitate the promotion of trade; this would help countries to take advantage of the new trade opportunities. But the issue is whether to expand its six priority areas[4] to cover the infrastructure for protecting intellectual property rights, managing dumping enquiries and so on, where technical assistance is urgently needed. This would require a new, dedicated, programme and additional resources.[5]

D. *International financial institutions*

The Final Act notes that the World Bank and the IMF's facilities may provide the resources needed for net food importing countries to cover the increased short-term costs of commercial food imports and to address the social costs of trade liberalization. To date, the Bank and the IMF consider existing facilities to be sufficient for this purpose (see, for example, IMF, 1994, Vol. I, p. 4; GATT, 1994b, p. 10). In the case of the IMF, the preferred instruments are the Extended Fund Facility for balance-of-payments support, and the Enhanced Structural Adjustment Facility for medium-term adjustment. The Compensatory and Contingency Financing Facility is considered by the Fund to be too short-term to deal

with the adjustments expected in the Uruguay Round. But only 19 of the countries shown in table 1 currently have active IMF programmes. And even these may not want to increase their use of IMF debt-creating, and conditional, resources - or they may not be able to do so. Moreover, it would be inappropriate to make compensation conditional in this way (FAO, 1995, p. 10).

The World Bank could provide technical assistance, especially in trade promotion and labour adjustment programmes, as well as in the development of domestic food supplies. Bank/Fund coordination is clearly imperative, both in monitoring individual countries' needs (to be coordinated with the WTO and the OECD Development Assistance Committee) and in providing financial and technical assistance. There is some history of this, with both providing finances in connection with trade reforms (Calika and Corsepius, 1994, p. 78). One possibility would be the creation of a Trade Adjustment Assistance facility or programme, with grant or very soft terms. This would have a broader mandate than the FAO's proposed food financing facility, in that it would cover losses on the export side arising from reduced preferences, increased costs of technology and other products resulting from the tougher intellectual property provisions, infrastructure needs, and finance for food.

Conclusions

It appears that many studies on the impact of the Round expect that the short-term costs to the poorest countries will be marginal and that they will be offset to some extent by their own economic restructuring and expansion of exports in the medium-term. But there is some recognition that many of these countries are already in severe financial difficulties and unable to cope with additional economic losses. Moreover, their economic restructuring will be a lengthy and resource-intensive process. In contrast, the benefits of the Round for the developed countries (and some of the more advanced developing countries) are much less ambiguous. They should therefore live up to the spirit of their commitments in the Final Act to increase assistance - both bilaterally and multilaterally - to the poorest countries in compensation for their losses and to ease their adjustment.

Should the various commitments to technical assistance and other forms of financial compensation made in the course of the Round fail to materialize, developing countries should consider using the dispute settlement procedures of the WTO, with the ultimate possibility of revising (and reversing) their own commitments. For instance, a least developed country might postpone its enforcement of intellectual property rights or reduce its bindings on services if a dispute panel found that developed countries had failed to give it substantially increased technical assistance in export diversification or improved preferential tariff access.

Notes

1 These numbers are not strictly comparable for various reasons - they are drawn from studies which use different models, and have different base and end years. Some use estimates rather than the Round's actual negotiated results, and even in the case of the latest papers there is not one which covers the full set of Uruguay Round agreements (Francois et al., 1995, p.11).

2 These calculations (FAO, 1995, table 3) are derived from the GATT's projected $200 billion increase in global income, coupled with agreed cuts in agricultural tariffs and export subsidies, but not domestic subsidies.

3 It has been recognized that "this work should be strengthened and its effectiveness increased, in order to better respond to the needs of developing countries resulting from their increased participation in the GATT system, from the complexity of the instruments negotiated within the framework of the Uruguay Round, and from the implementation of the results after its conclusion" (GATT, 1994b, p. 111).

4 Trade development strategy and programme design, trade information, export product and market development, development of trade support services, import management, and human resource development.

5 ITC funding in 1994 was $39.8 million, i.e. 29 per cent below its 1990 level. Almost a third is in the form of voluntary trust funds, often on a yearly basis, making programme planning difficult.

References

CALIKA, Nur, and Uwe CORSEPIUS (1994), "Trade Reforms in Fund-Supported Programs", in IMF (1994), *Volume II*.

DEGBELO, Jacques, and Paul DEMBINSKI (1994), "Effets de l'Uruguay Round sur les pays en développement: une analyse des évaluations realisées à ce jour" (Geneva: Ecodiagnostic), November.

DEROSA, Dean A. (1994), "The Uruguay Round Agreement on Agriculture and Sub-Saharan Africa", paper presented at the Workshop on the Role of Agriculture in Promoting Sustainable Economic Development in Africa, 30 October - 3 November, Neuchâtel, Switzerland.

FAO (1995), Committee on World Food Security, "Assessment of the Current World Food Security Situation And Medium Term Review", Rome, CFS 95/2.

FRANCOIS, Joseph F., Bradley MCDONALD and Håkan NORDSTRÖM (1995), "Assessing the Uruguay Round",
paper presented at the World Bank Conference on the Uruguay Round and the Developing Economies, 26-27 January, Washington, D.C..

GATT (1994a), "Developing Countries and the Uruguay Round: An Overview", Note by the Secretariat, Geneva, 10 November.

GATT (1994b), *Activities 1993* (Geneva).

GOLDIN, Ian, and Dominique VAN DER MENSBRUGGHE (1995), "The Uruguay Round: An Assessment of Economywide and Agricultural Reforms", paper presented at the World Bank Conference on the Uruguay Round and the Developing Economies, 26-27 January, Washington, D.C..

HARMSEN, Richard, and Arvind SUBRAMANIAN (1994), "Economic Implications of the Uruguay Round", in IMF (1994), *Volume II*.

HARRISON, Glenn W., Thomas F. RUTHERFORD, and David G. TARR (1995), "Quantifying the Uruguay Round", paper presented at the World Bank Conference on the Uruguay Round and the Developing Economies, 26-27 January, Washington, D.C..

HARROLD, Peter (1995), "The Impact of the Uruguay Round on Africa: Much Ado About Nothing?", paper presented at the World Bank Conference on The Uruguay Round and the Developing Economies, 26-27 January, Washington, D.C..

HATHAWAY, Dale E., and Merlinda D. INGCO (1995), "Agricultural Liberalization and the Uruguay Round", paper presented at the World Bank Conference on the Uruguay Round and the Developing Economies, 26-27 January, Washington, D.C..

HERTEL, Thomas, Will MARTIN, Koji YANAGISHIMA, and Betina DIMARANAN (1995), "Liberalizing Manufactures Trade in a Changing World Economy", paper presented at the World Bank Conference on the Uruguay Round and the Developing Economies, 26-27 January, Washington, D.C..

INGCO, Merlinda D. (1995), "Agricultural Trade Liberalization in the Uruguay Round: One Step Forward, One Step Back?", paper presented at the World Bank Conference on the Uruguay Round and the Developing Economies, 26-27 January, Washington D.C..

IMF (1994), *International Trade Policies. The Uruguay Round and Beyond. Volume I: Principal Issues. Volume II: Background Papers* (Washington D.C.).

ITC (1994), *ITC at the Crossroads: An Agenda for the Future* (Geneva), 5 October.

OECD (1994), Development Assistance Committee, *Development Cooperation 1994* (Paris).

PAGE, Sheila, and Michael DAVENPORT (1994), *World Trade Reform. Do Developing Countries Gain or Lose?* (London: Overseas Development Institute).

PRIMO BRAGA, Carlos A. (1995), "Trade-Related Intellectual Property Issues: The Uruguay Round Agreement and its Economic Implications", paper presented at the World Bank Conference on the Uruguay Round and the Developing Economies, 26-27 January, Washington, D.C..

SCHOTT, Jeffrey (1994), assisted by Johanna BUURMAN, *The Uruguay Round. An Assessment*, (Washington D.C.: Institute for International Economics).

STEVENS, Christopher, and Jane KENNAN (1994), *How will the EU's response to the GATT Round affect developing countries?* (Sussex: Institute for Development Studies).

UNDP/UNCTAD (1994), *Evaluation of the Final Results of the Uruguay Round by African Countries* (Geneva), 28 April.

UNCTAD (1994), *Trade and Development Report, 1994* (New York: United Nations Publication, Sales No. E.94.II.D.26).

UNCTAD (1995), *Translating Uruguay Round special provisions for least developed countries into concrete action: issues and policy requirements* (Geneva), March.

WESTON, Ann (1995), "The Uruguay Round: Unravelling the Implications for the Least Developed and Low-income Countries", in UNCTAD, *International Monetary and Financial Issues for the 1990s*, Vol. VI (UNCTAD/GID/G24/6)(New York and Geneva: United Nations).